Instructor's Manual and Test Bank to Accompany

The Moral of the Story

An Introduction to Questions of Ethics and Human Nature

Nina Rosenstand
San Diego State University

Mayfield Publishing Company
Mountain View, California
London • Toronto

International Standard Book Number: 1-55934-028-2

Manufactured in the United States of America
10 9 8 7 6 5 4 3 2 1

Mayfield Publishing Company
1280 Villa Street
Mountain View, CA 94041

 This book is printed on recycled paper.

CONTENTS

PREFACE

In writing this manual accompanying *The Moral of the Story*, I've set out to accomplish two things: (1) to provide you with a "road map" to the text, including suggestions for further class discussions, and (2) to make available to you a set of suggested test questions.

The Moral of the Story is an introduction to ethical theory, written primarily for college courses covering subjects such as "Introduction to Philosophy: Values," "Introduction to Ethics," and "Moral Problems." The book has four major parts, and the fourth part may also serve as an independent text for courses at colleges and universities in "Philosophy of Human Nature/Philosophy of Man." In addition, *The Moral of the Story* contains sections on philosophy and literature that may be used as a supplementary text in a "Literature and Philosophy" course.

While many textbooks in value theory/ethics present problems of social importance for students to discuss, such as abortion, euthanasia, and capital punishment, I find it is better to introduce students to basic ethical theory before they plunge into discussions involving moral judgments. The main focus of this book is thus an overview of some classical and modern approaches to ethical theory, such as ethical relativism, egoism, utilitarianism, deontology, and virtue theory, and a selection of influential theories about human nature.

However, because I believe that a full understanding of any ethical theory is possible only through the application of that theory to specific cases, I have chosen numerous examples to illustrate the theories in question. Over the years I have experimented with showing films and reading fiction as part of a philosophy course, and I have come to believe that one of the best ways to illustrate ethical theory is through the use of *fiction*. My own students usually respond very well to this approach. Besides, it has been a particularly gratifying experience for me to use literature/film in conjunction with philosophy in the classroom in a combination of theory and practice that is novel to the student. I hope that you too may find this experience both refreshing and rewarding.

Incidentally, just in case any student should misunderstand my meaning, you might mention that the Noel Coward quote on page iv of the main text is heavy irony. The line is made fun of by the three main characters of the play: the woman and her two lovers, a playwright and a painter living in a *ménage à trois* (supposedly platonic) in an artist's apartment in Paris. Ernest Lubitch made it into a film in 1933 with Gary Cooper, Fredric March, Miriam Hopkins, and Edward Everett Horton (speaking the quoted line), and it is still worth watching. You may want to discuss with your students whether the quote has merit or not, regardless of Coward's intention.

A BRIEF OVERVIEW OF THE TEXT

The Moral of the Story has four major sections: Part 1 introduces the topic of ethics and places the phenomenon of storytelling within a context of cross-cultural moral education and discussion. Part 2 examines the conduct theories of ethical relativism, psychological and ethical egoism, utilitarianism, and Kantian deontology. Part 3 explores the topic of virtue theory in chapters on Plato, Aristotle, theories of virtues and values of non-Western/noncontemporary traditions, and contemporary virtue theories in the Anglo-American tradition as well as in continental philosophy. Part 4 focuses on the question of ethics in relation to theories of human nature; topics discussed are theories of personhood, determinism and freedom of the will, gender theories, theories of good and evil human nature, and theories of humans as social, psychological, and storytelling beings.

    The Moral of the Story additionally contains three chapters with outlines of narratives, followed by study questions; Chapter 7 concludes the section on theory of conduct, Chapter 13 concludes the section on virtue theory, and Chapter 20 concludes the section on human nature. I have chosen to gather all the narratives in separate chapters instead of placing the stories directly behind the theoretical section because it facilitates the discussion; in this way, each story may serve as an illustration of several different theories. Each narrative outline is marked with an icon signifying whether the story is a novel, a short story, a film, a television show, a play, or a poem; several of the stories are marked with several different icons: The first icon signifies which story format the outline is based on, and the following icon(s) tell if there are other formats to this story. Example: Shakespeare's *Othello* is marked by the icon for "book," but it carries a secondary icon signifying "film." Only the most important alternative media versions of a story are marked by secondary icons; thus, if a well-known film is based on a book that has not had the same impact, only the film icon is displayed.

Readings

The Moral of the Story contains extensive citations from classical texts that will provide students with sufficient material to discuss the theories and give them a clear impression of the philosopher's style. However, there are few lengthy excerpts of primary text; I decided to avoid such selections because I've found that a difficult primary text often may cause the inexperienced student to "lose heart" and give up on philosophy. Should you want to supplement this text with a selection of primary texts, there are several excellent anthologies available.

SOME SUGGESTIONS ON HOW TO USE
THE NARRATIVE SECTIONS

I chose the narratives in Chapters 1, 7, 13, and 20 from a wide variety of cross-cultural sources. From a literary and artistic point of view these outlines of course don't do the originals justice; a story worth experiencing, be it a novel, a short story, or a film, cannot be reduced to a mere plot outline and still retain all of its essence. Furthermore, there is usually more to the story than the bare bones of a moral problem, and in writing these outlines I have had to disregard much of the richness of story and character development. Nevertheless, I have chosen the outline format in order to be able to discuss a number of different stories and genres as they relate to specific issues in ethics; and because I believe it is important to show that there is a cross-cultural, historic tradition of exploring moral problems through telling a story, I have opted for a broad selection of narrative outlines.

Each theoretical chapter in *The Moral of the Story* has a number of corresponding stories in the narrative chapters, and at the end of each chapter you will find a specification of which stories in the concluding chapter of narratives are relevant as discussion material. Not all themes in the book are illustrated by narrative examples—that would have been an overwhelming task; however, if you find that a theme should be emphasized further by adding an outline of a narrative you are familiar with, I would appreciate your suggestions.

It is not my intention that you should go through all these stories with the students. Except in the case where *The Moral of the Story* is used specifically in a class focusing on literature and philosophy, few philosophy instructors will have enough time set aside to go into detail with more than a few narratives; however, the book is designed so that you can choose one or two stories to illustrate each theoretical problem.

Each narrative or group of narratives has a few study questions at the end. These questions are not intended to exhaust the discussion topic; rather, their purpose is to get a discussion started.

Although most students relate immediately to the idea of applying questions of value and moral issues to stories, a few students may never have been exposed to the idea that a story may be telling more than its actual plot. I have found through experience that the idea of symbolism or metaphor in a story is completely unfamiliar to a small percentage of students, and before embarking on an ethical analysis of the stories in this book you might do well to spend a few minutes explaining to the students that stories have several levels: a story-line level and any number of levels where the author "speaks between the lines," addressing philosophical, psychological, social, political, or other issues. In much popular fiction these levels tend to be at a minimum, whereas in what is known as "higher literature" such levels may be numerous.

The following list contains three examples of how you might use the narrative selections:

EXAMPLE 1: ETHICAL RELATIVISM

Chapter 3: Ethical Relativism
> plus Chapter 7: *Do the Right Thing* and *Sideshow*
> *or* Chapter 7: *The Last of the Mohicans* and *A Passage to India*
> *or* Chapter 7: *Lawrence of Arabia* and *Sideshow*

EXAMPLE 2: UTILITARIANISM VS. KANTIANISM

Chapter 5: Utilitarianism and Chapter 6: Kant's Deontology
> plus Chapter 7: "The Blacksmith and the Baker," *Abandon Ship!*, and *High Noon*
> *or* Chapter 7: *The Brothers Karamazov* and "The Ones Who Walk Away from Omelas"
> *or* Chapter 7: *Abandon Ship!*, *Rebel Without a Cause*, and *Star Trek: The Next Generation:* "Justice"

EXAMPLE 3: WHAT IS A PERSON?

Chapter 14: What Is a Person?
> plus Chapter 20: *Pinocchio* and *Star Trek: The Next Generation:* "The Measure of a Man"
> *or* Chapter 20: *Orphan of Creation* and *Star Trek: The Next Generation:* "The Measure of a Man"
> *or* Chapter 20: *Blade Runner* and "The Circular Ruins"

I usually discuss the story *after* going over the theoretical chapter with my students, but you may want to incorporate the story into the theoretical discussion itself.

There are, of course, many other ways in which stories and ethical theory can be brought together. You might, for instance, select one or two short stories or films in their original format for class discussion; I hope that you will indeed select a few stories—a novel, a short story, or a video—for your students to experience firsthand.[*] However, the outlines are written so that a firsthand experience should not be necessary for a discussion of the problem presented by the story; the outlines give the students just enough information to engage in a discussion of the moral problem presented. It is my hope that some students might actually become inspired to seek out the originals on their own—I am happy to report this being the case with many of my own students.

Because space is limited, I have not been able to include more than a sampling of stories, and I readily admit that the criteria of choice are my own; I find them interesting

---

[*] Please note that copyright restrictions apply to the showing of videos in a classroom situation. Your school should be able to inform you of current copyright regulations.

as illustrations and effective in a classroom context where students come from many different cultural backgrounds. I selected the stories on the basis of their clarity in presenting moral problems, not from any evaluation of their quality as enduring classics nor from any grand plan of systematically representing all aspects of world literature. You might choose other stories, and even choose completely different ethical problems to be illustrated, and I would be delighted to hear from you how this selection of stories might be expanded and improved. Most of the narratives are available in libraries, bookstores, and video or laser disc rental stores (for private viewing).

For a viewpoint that is squarely opposed to this approach of using stories in ethics you may want to examine a book by Peter Thorpe, *Why Literature Is Bad for You* (Chicago: Nelson-Hall, 1980). In his book, Thorpe argues that authors and literature professors are a small and mentally rather deviant minority that doesn't represent the moral values of the majority: They oversimplify moral problems, make their readers and students lazy and self-centered, and make them tolerant of incompetence, and above all, authors have invented the generation gap that didn't exist before they started writing about it. In addition, Thorpe seems to believe novels should be read mainly as plot outlines, if at all. As you can probably tell, I disagree with most of his arguments, but the book is provocative and entertaining.

In the next section, on course material, there will be listings of a few additional narratives in case you wish to explore the subject further with your class. However, if you prefer to use this book strictly with emphasis on ethical theory without using stories as examples, the three chapters on narratives can be bypassed without loss of theoretical content.

ALTERNATIVE TEACHING SCENARIOS

The Moral of the Story is designed to accommodate several different teaching scenarios. The ideal scenario of two leisurely semesters (which must unfortunately remain a fantasy for most philosophy instructors) would allow for reading the entire text with the class, but here I have outlined strategy options for (1) a semester schedule and (2) a quarter schedule.

Depending on your preference for topics within the general subject of ethics, you might select one of the following possible approaches:

ONE SEMESTER (16–18 WEEKS)

1. *Focus on classical conduct and virtue theories.*

   Chapter 1: Who Cares About Ethics?
   Chapter 2: Stories in Our Lives
   Chapter 3: Ethical Relativism (with selected narratives from Chapter 7)
   Chapter 4: Myself or Others? (with selected narratives from Chapter 7)
   Chapter 5: Using Your Reason, Part 1: Utilitarianism (with selected narratives from Chapter 7)
   Chapter 6: Using Your Reason, Part 2: Kant's Deontology (with selected narratives from Chapter 7)
   Chapter 8: Socrates, Plato, and the Good Life
   Chapter 9: Aristotle's Virtue Theory (with selected narratives from Chapter 13)
   Chapter 10: Virtues and Values of Other Traditions (with selected narratives from Chapter 13)
   Chapter 11: The Modern Perspective (with selected narratives from Chapter 13)
   Chapter 12: Case Studies in Virtue (with selected narratives from Chapter 13)

2. *Focus on conduct and virtue theories with emphasis on a contemporary aspect.*

   Chapter 1: Who Cares About Ethics?
   Chapter 2: Stories in Our Lives
   Chapter 3: Ethical Relativism (with selected narratives from Chapter 7)
   Chapter 4: Myself or Others? (with selected narratives from Chapter 7)
   Chapter 5: Using Your Reason, Part 1: Utilitarianism (with selected narratives from Chapter 7)
   Chapter 6: Using Your Reason, Part 2: Kant's Deontology (with selected narratives from Chapter 7)
   Chapter 8: Socrates, Plato, and the Good Life (introduction only)
   Chapter 11: The Modern Perspective (with selected narratives from Chapter 13)
   Chapter 12: Case Studies in Virtue (with selected narratives from Chapter 13)
   Chapter 14: What Is a Person? (with selected narratives from Chapter 20)
   Chapter 16: Different Gender, Different Nature, Different Ethics? (with selected narratives from Chapter 20)
   Chapter 19: The Storytelling Animal

3. *Focus on a cross-cultural perspective.*
   Chapter 1: Who Cares About Ethics?
   Chapter 2: Stories in Our Lives
   Chapter 3: Ethical Relativism (with selected narratives from Chapter 7)
   Chapter 4: Myself or Others? (with selected narratives from Chapter 7)
   Chapter 5: Using Your Reason, Part 1: Utilitarianism (with selected narratives from Chapter 7)
   Chapter 6: Using Your Reason, Part 2: Kant's Deontology (with selected narratives from Chapter 7)
   Chapter 8: Socrates, Plato, and the Good Life
   Chapter 9: Aristotle's Virtue Theory (with selected narratives from Chapter 13)
   Chapter 10: Virtues and Values of Other Traditions (with selected narratives from Chapter 13)
   Chapter 14: What Is a Person? (with selected narratives from Chapter 20)
   Chapter 16: Different Gender, Different Nature, Different Ethics? (with selected narratives from Chapter 20)

4. *Focus on narrative theory and ethics.*
   Chapter 1: Who Cares About Ethics?
   Chapter 2: Stories in Our Lives
   Chapter 3: Ethical Relativism (with selected narratives from Chapter 7)
   Chapter 4: Myself or Others? (with selected narratives from Chapter 7)
   Chapter 5: Using Your Reason, Part 1: Utilitarianism (with selected narratives from Chapter 7)
   Chapter 6: Using Your Reason, Part 2: Kant's Deontology (with selected narratives from Chapter 7)
   Chapter 8: Socrates, Plato, and the Good Life
   Chapter 9: Aristotle's Virtue Theory (with selected narratives from Chapter 13)
   Chapter 10: Virtues and Values of Other Traditions (with selected narratives from Chapter 13)
   Chapter 11: The Modern Perspective (with selected narratives from Chapter 13)
   Chapter 12: Case Studies in Virtue (with selected narratives from Chapter 13)
   Chapter 19: The Storytelling Animal

5. *Focus on theories of human nature.*
   Chapter 3: Ethical Relativism (with selected narratives from Chapter 7)
   Chapter 4: Myself or Others? (with selected narratives from Chapter 7)
   Chapter 5: Using Your Reason, Part 1: Utilitarianism (with selected narratives from Chapter 7)
   Chapter 6: Using Your Reason, Part 2: Kant's Deontology (with selected narratives from Chapter 7)
   Chapter 10: Virtues and Values of Other Traditions (with selected narratives from Chapter 13)

Chapter 14: What Is a Person? (with selected narratives from Chapter 20)

Chapter 15: Can We Decide Our Own Actions? (with selected narratives from Chapter 20)

Chapter 16: Different Gender, Different Nature, Different Ethics? (with selected narratives from Chapter 20)

Chapter 17: Are We Good or Evil from the Beginning? (with selected narratives from Chapter 20)

Chapter 18: The Soul and the State (with selected narratives from Chapter 20)

Chapter 19: The Storytelling Animal

6. *Focus on gender-related issues.*

Chapter 1: Who Cares About Ethics?

Chapter 2: Stories in Our Lives

Chapter 14: What Is a Person? (with selected narratives from Chapter 20)

Chapter 15: Can We Decide Our Own Actions? (with selected narratives from Chapter 20)

Chapter 16: Different Gender, Different Nature, Different Ethics? (with selected narratives from Chapter 20)

Chapter 5: Using Your Reason, Part 1: Utilitarianism (with selected narratives from Chapter 7)

Chapter 6: Using Your Reason, Part 2: Kant's Deontology (with selected narratives from Chapter 7)

Chapter 8: Socrates, Plato, and the Good Life

Chapter 9: Aristotle's Virtue Theory (with selected narratives from Chapter 13)

Chapter 10: Virtues and Values of Other Traditions (with selected narratives from Chapter 13)

Chapter 11: The Modern Perspective (with selected narratives from Chapter 13)

Chapter 12: Case Studies in Virtue (with selected narratives from Chapter 13)

Chapter 19: The Storytelling Animal

7. *A historical approach.* (Such a selection is not part of the book's design, but it is an option to piece together a strictly historical approach. This selection excludes the narrative chapters, but you can of course browse through the narrative sections and select stories that will accommodate a historical approach.)

Chapter 8: Socrates, Plato, and the Good Life

Chapter 9: Aristotle's Virtue Theory

Chapter 18: The Soul and the State (Plato and Aristotle sections)

Chapter 10: Virtues and Values of Other Traditions

Chapter 17: Are We Good or Evil from the Beginning? (Augustine, Hobbes, and Rousseau sections)

Chapter 5: Using Your Reason, Part 1: Utilitarianism

Chapter 6: Using Your Reason, Part 2: Kant's Deontology

Chapter 17: Are We Good or Evil from the Beginning? (Nietzsche section)

Chapter 18: The Soul and the State (Marx and Freud sections)

Chapter 11: The Modern Perspective
Chapter 12: Case Studies in Virtue
Chapter 16: Different Gender, Different Nature, Different Ethics?

ONE QUARTER (10 WEEKS)

For the time pressure of the quarter system I suggest limiting the narrative illustrations to one story per theoretical chapter.

1. *Focus on classical conduct and virtue theories.*
   Chapter 1: Who Cares About Ethics?
   Chapter 3: Ethical Relativism (with one selected narrative from Chapter 7)
   Chapter 4: Myself or Others? (with one selected narrative from Chapter 7)
   Chapter 5: Using Your Reason, Part 1: Utilitarianism (with one selected narrative from Chapter 7)
   Chapter 6: Using Your Reason, Part 2: Kant's Deontology (with one selected narrative from Chapter 7)
   Chapter 8: Socrates, Plato, and the Good Life
   Chapter 9: Aristotle's Virtue Theory (with one selected narrative from Chapter 13)

2. *Focus on conduct and virtue theories with emphasis on a contemporary aspect.*
   Chapter 1: Who Cares About Ethics?
   Chapter 3: Ethical Relativism (with one selected narrative from Chapter 7)
   Chapter 4: Myself or Others? (with one selected narrative from Chapter 7)
   Chapter 5: Using Your Reason, Part 1: Utilitarianism (with one selected narrative from Chapter 7)
   Chapter 6: Using Your Reason, Part 2: Kant's Deontology (with one selected narrative from Chapter 7)
   Chapter 8: Socrates, Plato, and the Good Life (introduction only)
   Chapter 11: The Modern Perspective (with one selected narrative from Chapter 13)
   Chapter 14: What Is a Person? (with one selected narrative from Chapter 20)
   Chapter 16: Different Gender, Different Nature, Different Ethics? (with one selected narrative from Chapter 20)

3. *Focus on a cross-cultural perspective.*
   Chapter 1: Who Cares About Ethics?
   Chapter 3: Ethical Relativism (with one selected narrative from Chapter 7)
   Chapter 5: Using Your Reason, Part 1: Utilitarianism (with one selected narrative from Chapter 7)
   Chapter 6: Using Your Reason, Part 2: Kant's Deontology (with one selected narrative from Chapter 7)
   Chapter 8: Socrates, Plato, and the Good Life

Chapter 10: Virtues and Values of Other Traditions (with one selected narrative from Chapter 13)

Chapter 14: What Is a Person? (with one selected narrative from Chapter 20)

4. *Focus on narrative theory and ethics.*

Chapter 1: Who Cares About Ethics?

Chapter 2: Stories in Our Lives

Chapter 5: Using Your Reason, Part 1: Utilitarianism (with one selected narrative from Chapter 7)

Chapter 6: Using Your Reason, Part 2: Kant's Deontology (with one selected narrative from Chapter 7)

Chapter 8: Socrates, Plato, and the Good Life

Chapter 9: Aristotle's Virtue Theory (with one selected narrative from Chapter 13)

Chapter 11: The Modern Perspective (with one selected narrative from Chapter 13)

Chapter 19: The Storytelling Animal

5. *Focus on theories of human nature.*

Chapter 3: Ethical Relativism (with one selected narrative from Chapter 7)

Chapter 4: Myself or Others? (with one selected narrative from Chapter 7)

Chapter 14: What Is a Person? (with one selected narrative from Chapter 20)

Chapter 15: Can We Decide Our Own Actions? (with one selected narrative from Chapter 20)

Chapter 16: Different Gender, Different Nature, Different Ethics? (with one selected narrative from Chapter 20)

Chapter 17: Are We Good or Evil from the Beginning? (with two selected narratives from Chapter 20 for the theories of Hobbes and Rousseau)

Chapter 18: The Soul and the State (with two selected narratives from Chapter 20 for the theories of Marx and Freud)

Chapter 19: The Storytelling Animal

6. *Focus on gender-related issues.*

Chapter 5: Using Your Reason, Part 1: Utilitarianism (with one selected narrative from Chapter 7)

Chapter 6: Using Your Reason, Part 2: Kant's Deontology (with one selected narrative from Chapter 7)

Chapter 14: What Is a Person? (with one selected narrative from Chapter 20)

Chapter 16: Different Gender, Different Nature, Different Ethics? (with one selected narrative from Chapter 20)

Chapter 8: Socrates, Plato, and the Good Life (introduction only)

Chapter 10: Virtues and Values of Other Traditions (with one selected narrative from Chapter 13)

Chapter 11: The Modern Perspective (with one selected narrative from
    Chapter 13)
Chapter 19: The Storytelling Animal

7. *A historical approach.* (Please see comment for the 18-week course.)
    Chapter 8: Socrates, Plato, and the Good Life
    Chapter 9: Aristotle's Virtue Theory
    Chapter 10: Virtues and Values of Other Traditions
    Chapter 17: Are We Good or Evil from the Beginning? (Augustine, Hobbes, and
        Rousseau sections)
    Chapter 5: Using Your Reason, Part 1: Utilitarianism
    Chapter 6: Using Your Reason, Part 2: Kant's Deontology
    Chapter 17: Are We Good or Evil from the Beginning? (Nietzsche section)
    Chapter 11: The Modern Perspective
    Chapter 16: Different Gender, Different Nature, Different Ethics?

CLASS PRESENTATION MATERIALS: A DETAILED OVERVIEW*

Part 1: The Story as a Tool of Ethics

Part 1 defines the concepts of ethics, morals, and values, and it introduces the narrative as one medium through which morals may be taught and discussed.

Chapter 1: Who Cares About Ethics?

This introductory chapter outlines the growing interest in moral issues. The terminology of ethics, morals, and values is introduced and discussed, and the discussion focuses on different groups in society showing an interest in ethical issues (such as religious groups, the media, the medical world, the scientific world, and the entertainment industry). Three major approaches to moral problems are introduced: ethical relativism, hard universalism, and soft universalism. Examples of moral dilemmas ("scruples") are provided, courtesy of several students of mine, and in this opening chapter we meet for the first time examples of ethics in narratives; three films are used as examples of how a story might explore a moral problem: *Altered States*, *Working Girl*, and *Network*.

Main Points

Ethics, Morals, and Values

- The difference between ethics and morals: Morality refers to moral rules we follow, whereas ethics refers to theories about these rules—questioning and justifying the rules.

SUGGESTION

You may want to ask your students whether they would have different expectations of the course if it were titled "Introduction to Morals" or "Introduction to Ethics" or "Values." Most students will, instinctively, perceive a "morals" course to be somehow restrictive.

- The concept of values: Only philosophy can evaluate whether people's values are justified.
- Should schools teach values? Because we live in a multicultural society it is better for schools to focus on ethics rather than on specific moral rules.

Who Thinks Ethics Is Important?

- Philosophy: Ethics is one of the major branches of philosophical inquiry.

---

* This section contains boxes with suggestions for further discussion. In most cases, the boxes contain discussion material in addition to the themes explored in the text, not as a listing of all discussion topics.

- The church: For many people ethics and religion are inseparable, but it is possible to have secular ethical standards.
- Medicine: The accomplishments of medical research make it necessary to develop a new kind of ethical responsibility.
- Science: Scientific research needs to be aware of an ethical dimension: Just because something is possible, does it mean science has to do it?

- Business: The business world is becoming increasingly aware of ethical requirements and standards.
- The news media: Journalists must be aware of the ethics of reporting a news story.
- Legislation: Morals and laws do not always coincide, although the law usually follows public opinion.
- The entertainment industry: The preoccupation with moral issues in the entertainment industry often focuses on sex. There is a need for the entertainment industry to be responsible, especially in telling stories of violence.
- Storytellers: People sometimes tell stories to make a moral point.

Why Have Rules of Moral Conduct?

- The basic questions: Is morality a matter of the heart, or does it come from reason? Is morality a biological fail-safe, and are we all egoists at heart? How should one solve moral dilemmas?

Ethics in Narratives

- The plot outlines in *The Moral of the Story* have two purposes: (1) to supply a foundation for discussion, and (2) to inspire the students to experience the stories in their original form.

Science and Ethics

- Frankenstein's monster is the prototype of all stories in which science has disregarded moral values. The narrative used here to illustrate the issue is the film *Altered States* (1980): An anthropologist experiments with drugs in order to explore the topic of mind expansion, but finds that he is losing his own humanity in the process.

SOME ADDITIONAL NARRATIVES ILLUSTRATING
THE THEME OF SCIENCE AND ETHICS*
The theme of the "mad scientist," or research without a conscience for the sake of knowledge or profit, is covered in numerous works of literature and films. Some suggestions are:

Dr. Jekyll and Mr. Hyde (1886). The story is outlined in Chapter 20 as an illustration of good and evil human nature.

The Fly, film (1956, remade 1986).

The China Syndrome, film (1979).

Wild Palms, television miniseries (1993).

Jurassic Park, film (1993).

Business Ethics

- The issue of business ethics is illustrated by the film *Working Girl* (1988). A young secretary's idea is stolen by her boss, and the secretary embarks on an impersonation scheme, playing a business executive in the hope that her idea may be accepted.

SOME ADDITIONAL NARRATIVES ILLUSTRATING
THE THEME OF BUSINESS ETHICS

Henrik Ibsen, *A Doll's House*, play (1879). Made into a film by two different British film companies in 1973, one of the versions starring Jane Fonda.

Berthold Brecht, *Threepenny Opera*, play (1928).

---

*Throughout this manual you will find a selection of suggestions for additional stories to discuss. Titles may appear several times, as they can be used to illustrate several different moral problems. In these selections of additional stories I have chosen primarily "mainstream" stories, usually available through bookstores and/or video rental outlets. The order of titles is chronological.

Arthur Miller, *Death of a Salesman*, play (1948). Made into a film 1951 and 1985.

Save the Tiger, film (1973).

Wall Street, film (1987).

Glengarry Glen Ross, film (1992).

Just about any episode of the television series "Dallas."

Ethics and the Media

- The question of ethics in the media is illustrated by the film *Network* (1976). A television executive engages a group of terrorists to perform on-camera acts of terrorism in order to boost ratings.

OTHER NARRATIVES ILLUSTRATING
THE THEME OF ETHICS AND THE MEDIA

Front Page (1931, 1974).

His Girl Friday, film (1940). The same story as *Front Page*, except in *Front Page* the lead character is a man, and in *His Girl Friday* it is a woman.

Citizen Kane, film (1941).

Heinrich Böll, *The Lost Honor of Katharina Blum*, novel (1974). Made into a film 1975.

All the President's Men, film (1976).

The China Syndrome, film (1979).

Under Fire, film (1983).

Broadcast News, film (1987).

SUGGESTION

There is a whole category of fiction exploring the professional ethics of the characters in the story, all the way from ethics among architects, doctors, and lawyers, to "honor among thieves." If the students are receptive, you may want to explore this theme further. A few examples are: *The Fountainhead* (novel), *Rio Bravo* (film), *The Professionals* (film), *The Godfather* (film), *A Few Good Men* (film).

Boxes

Family Values   Discusses the concept of family values from a conservative and a liberal view.

God and Values   Discusses the connection between ethics and religion.

Is There Such a Thing as Value-free Science?   Discusses the connection between scientific research and private interests, based on Jürgen Habermas's critique.

Some "Scruples"   A selection of moral dilemmas submitted by college students.

Chapter 2: Stories in Our Lives

This chapter introduces the idea that we often learn moral lessons from the stories we are exposed to at an early age as well as later in life. With a lot of examples from world literature and film this chapter explores the relationship between fact and fiction and looks at the way stories have been told in order to teach moral lessons, from ancient myths to novels, short stories, and films. We examine different genres of stories as they affect our moral outlook (such as Westerns, science fiction, and war stories). The power of the story serving as a role model for behavior is discussed, and three particularly powerful story types are examined: the bargain, the twins, and the quest.

Main Points

Learning Moral Lessons from Stories

- Powerful stories help children learn moral lessons, such as "The Boy Who Cried Wolf."
- Stories are increasingly recognized as moral tools by philosophers.
- Stories that moralize are contrasted with stories that tell an open-ended tale of moral problems.

Telling Stories

Fact, Fiction, or Both?

- Even factual stories are enriched with poetic creativity.

Stories with a Moral Lesson

- Myths: Storytelling of the beginning time of the culture, serving as moral explanations and roles to emulate.
- Fairy tales: Entertainment with an edge of wishful thinking.
- Parables: Religious allegories about the moral demands of God. Examples: "The Prodigal Son" and the story of Abraham and Isaac.
- Fables and counterfables: Moralizing (didactic) stories primarily for children.

Stories as Role Models

Who Are Our Heroes?

- Our heroes are not just good people, but we also learn lessons from "bad" people who mend their ways or "bad" people who are rightfully punished.

SUGGESTION

Your students may enjoy being asked to come up with titles of stories that are important to them. If some students cannot think of any, it may be an incentive for them to search for some stories they can relate to; they may well find such stories outside the mainstream of literature and film.

Some Contemporary Moral Lessons

- Moral lessons taught in older stories may not always have the same effect. Example: *Brave New World*.
- The following genres represent story types that often incorporate moral problems.

  Wartime ethics: Although war is no longer glorified, we may still enjoy hearing stories of the courage and loyalty of the soldier.

  The moral universe of Westerns: The moral potential of the Western has been utilized over the decades for different ideological purposes.

  Science fiction: This genre explores the moral problems in connection with topics such as genetic manipulation, environmental disasters, and artificial intelligence.

  Crime and suspense: The changing nature of crime-fighting stories shows a shift in interest from simple "who-dunnits" to tales of corruption among police officers.

Stories of Influence

Stories to Live and Die By

- Novels are capable of affecting the reader greatly. Example: Goethe's *The Sorrows of Werther*.
- Often the stories that affect us the most are those in which the hero has a flawed character, and the question often becomes whether such a person's life is somehow redeemed through the story.

Stories to Change the World

- Stories involving social criticism often have great effect on the world of the readers, such as *Gulliver's Travels, 1984*, and *The Trial*.

Some Fantastic Tales for Grown-ups

- Three story types in the Western tradition are here selected as archetypes of stories that humans continually relate to: *the bargain* (exemplified by the story of Dr. Faust who sells his soul to the Devil), *the twin motif* (stories of a good twin and an evil twin, symbolizing two sides to the human psyche) and *the quest* (the search for a treasure—from the ultimate treasure of immortality to the Holy Grail, and all the way to more mundane treasure hunts for money).

Boxes

Kafka's Abraham Discusses Franz Kafka's version of the Abraham legend.

War Movies with a Message Looks at war movies that try to remain as factual as possible and war movies that provide a looser historical interpretation.

The Changing Messages of Westerns Westerns have the capability of exploring current issues; the changing issues in the traditional and recent Westerns.

The Nonhuman Who Wants to Become Human The moral situation of the artificial human being who helps us identify what humanity is.

The Good Guys and the Bad Guys The moral confusion in suspense stories: cops as good and bad guys.

Do Slasher Movies Teach a Lesson? The hidden messages of slasher movies: life is cheap, and sex and death are somehow connected.

Fictional Friends Some examples of characters in books and films that have come to feel like personal friends to many.

Twin Souls in Books and Films The twin motif in Western narrative tradition, from actual twins to alter ego stories.

Looking for Love The quest for love in film and literature, and the dangers and disappointments.

The Holy Grail in the Movies A selection of films dealing with the quest for something vitally important.

Part 2: What Should I Do? Theories of Conduct

Part 2 examines the most influential theories of ethical conduct in Western philosophy.

Chapter 3: Ethical Relativism

This chapter explains the theory of ethical relativism. As an introductory issue the question of moral differences is discussed, leading up to the lesson taught by anthropology that morality is a matter of acculturation. The view of relativity is questioned, and it is contrasted to the approach of soft universalism. Finally, a discussion of cultural diversity outlines the pros and cons of ethical relativism.

Main Points

How to Deal with Moral Differences

- Four major ways to approach moral differences: (1) moral nihilism and skepticism, (2) ethical relativism, (3) soft universalism, and (4) hard universalism (absolutism).

The Lessons of Anthropology

- A presentation of the theories of cultural and ethical relativism, and an analysis of how they differ.
- King Darius compares Greek and Callatian funeral practices.
- According to the anthropologist Ruth Benedict, the concept of the normal is a variant of the concept of the good.

Is Tolerance All We Need?

- There are circumstances in which the tolerance of ethical relativism seems inappropriate, such as in cases of nations committing genocide on their own population.
- Relativism precludes learning from other cultures.
- Relativism acknowledges only majority rule.

SUGGESTION

As part of a discussion of the problem of majority identity in ethical relativism, you may want to ask your students to come up with examples of a majority population officially supporting one moral viewpoint and unofficially following another standard—the phenomenon we usually call a "double standard." Possible examples of such behavior may be sexual morals in different time periods (such as the Victorian era) and the ideal of honesty.

- There is a practical problem deciding what a majority is.

Refuting Ethical Relativism

The Nature of Moral Truths

The mere fact that there is cultural disagreement doesn't ascertain that no common ground can be found.

The Problem of Induction

The problem of induction (the fact that no absolute answer can be reached through empirical research) precludes relativism's rejection of a common moral ground.

Soft Universalism

- All cultures have at least some values in common, even if they express them in different ways.

The New Relativism of Cultural Diversity

- Exclusive multiculturalism (particularism) versus inclusive multiculturalism (pluralism).
- Inclusive multiculturalism can work as a form of soft universalism.

SUGGESTION _____

Many students have personal experiences with cultural diversity. You may want to ask for student contributions in the form of presentations or papers, asking their opinion on exclusive versus inclusive multiculturalism. You should expect a variety of presentations, some very personal and not necessarily of clearly defined philosophical content; however, a certain amount of leeway will probably be useful in order for students to be assured that their contribution and viewpoint are relevant, or at least can be shaped into a relevant philosophical argument. On occasion the classroom experience can become rather polarized during such presentations; not all students relate well to being exposed to the "differentness" of others, but I have found that the majority of students are genuinely open-minded and interested. You may want to open up the subject of multiculturalism and tolerance of practices that the majority find objectionable. This usually results in a lively discussion.

- Reference to Chapter 7 and story outlines concerning ethical relativism and cultural diversity: *Do the Right Thing*, *The Last of the Mohicans*, *A Passage to India*, *Lawrence of Arabia*, and *Sideshow*.

Boxes

Descriptive and Normative Ethics   Analyzes the difference between descriptive and normative ethics, and introduces the concept of metaethics.

The Psychology of Becoming a Moral and Social Being   Compares Benedict's concept of moral socialization with Freud's concept of the superego.

How to Test a Theory   Introduces the philosophical procedure of testing a theory to find its breaking point.

Cultural Diversity or Cultural Adversity?   Discusses the danger of assuming that the viewpoint of a group is wrong or right just by virtue of being held by the group: an *ad hominem* argument.

Chapter 4: Myself or Others?

Here we move to the classical question of egoism. First, the theory of psychological egoism is defined and discussed. Second, ethical egoism is presented and discussed, and the concept of consequentialism is introduced. Finally, the alternative of altruism is discussed.

Main Points

Psychological Egoism

Definition of the Theory

- A psychological, descriptive theory claiming that people behave selfishly.

SUGGESTION

While most philosophers take "ought implies can" to mean that something cannot be a duty if a person is unable to perform it, there is another possible meaning, explored by Johann Gottlieb Fichte: "If I ought, I can." In other words, if there is something I have to do, then I will be able to find a way to do it. Your students may enjoy discussing the difference between the two interpretations, and in particular whether there is any merit to Fichte's version.

All People Look After Themselves

- Plato's story of the Ring of Gyges.
- Three reasons why psychological egoism is popular: (1) appeal to honesty, (2) revisionist cynicism, and (3) an easy way to avoid considering the interests of others.

Shortcomings of Psychological Egoism

- The theory cannot be refuted.

SUGGESTION

Ask your students for contributions in the form of examples of altruistic deeds, and then proceed to dismiss them on the basis of psychological egoism. This is likely to convert your students to psychological egoism in a very short time, but here you may want to point out that this ability of psychological egoism to always get the last word is no advantage for a theory. Psychological egoism can be defeated only if attached in its foundational assumptions, not through empirical examples.

- Doing what you want is not always selfish. Example: Abraham Lincoln rescuing the pigs from the mud.
- A logical problem: The fallacy of the suppressed correlative.

Ethical Egoism

Definition of the Theory

- A normative theory about how we ought to behave: selfishly.

You Should Look After Yourself

- A version of the Golden Rule, with emphasis on oneself.
- Ethical egoism is a consequentialist theory.

The Shortcomings of Ethical Egoism

- Socrates's answer to Glaucon: A selfish person cannot be happy.
- The argument that ethical egoism is self-contradictory.
- The argument that ethical egoism works only if you advocate altruism while you yourself pursue egoism, but this cannot be universalized.

Altruism: Ideal and Real

- Cases of humans and animals sacrificing themselves for the good of others.
- Peter Singer's version of the Prisoner's Dilemma.

SUGGESTION

Your students may wonder about the classical formulation of the Prisoner's Dilemma, and here you'll find a brief outline of it (this clear version is presented by James Rachels in the second edition of *The Elements of Moral Reasoning*). You and Smith are both political prisoners of a totalitarian regime, and you are each told that the length of your sentence will depend on whether you confess or not. If you confess and Smith doesn't you will be sentenced to one year in prison and Smith will get ten years. If neither confesses, each will get two years. If both confess, each will get five years. If Smith confesses and you don't, Smith will get one year and you will get ten. If your only goal is to limit your own sentence, logic demands that you should confess, because you will be ahead whether or not Smith also confesses. However, since Smith is thinking along the same lines, chances are that, while looking out for your own interests, you will both confess and both get five years. However, if you think of Smith's interests also, and can be fairly certain that he (or she) is thinking of yours, then it will be to your mutual advantage: If you both don't confess, both will get out after two years only.

- Reference to Chapter 7 and story outlines concerning the issue of egoism: *Madame Bovary*, *Gone with the Wind*, and *Atlas Shrugged*.

Boxes

"Ought" Implies "Can"   Analyzes the meaning of the idea that we are not obliged to do something it is impossible for us to do.

Hobbes and the Feeling of Pity   Discusses Thomas Hobbes's idea that all emotions are reflections of self-love, including pity.

Hedonism   Introduces the concept of hedonism and the paradox of hedonism: The harder you seek pleasure, the more it eludes you.

SUGGESTION

You may want to discuss the implications of this old story with your students in connection with the hedonistic paradox: A Persian prince was told that in order to cure his unhappiness he had to wear the shirt of a happy man. The Persian prince now tried the shirts of lords, artists, merchants, fools, and soldiers, but it was to no avail. Happiness seemed to elude him. Finally he encountered a poor farmer singing behind his plow; the prince asked him if he was happy, and the farmer answered that he was. The prince then asked if he could have the farmer's shirt, and the farmer answered, "But I have no shirt!"

Falsification Must Be Theoretically Possible   Discusses Karl Popper's concept of the principle of falsification.

Lincoln: Humble Man or Clever Jokester?   Examines the possible reasons behind Lincoln's statement that he saved the pigs for selfish reasons.

Individual Ethical Egoism   Discusses and discards individual ethical egoism because it can't be universalized. Introduces universalizability.

David Hume: Humans Are Benevolent by Nature   Presents David Hume's theory of natural compassion.

Chapter 5: Using Your Reason, Part 1: Utilitarianism

Here utilitarianism is introduced as an alternative consequentialist theory through Bentham's concept of the hedonistic calculus. The advantages and disadvantages of the universe of utilitarianism are explored, and J. S. Mill's redefinition of utilitarianism in terms of higher and lower pleasures is discussed. Furthermore, Mill's harm principle is introduced, and the development from act to rule utilitarianism is briefly discussed.

Main Points

- Definition of the principle of utility.
- Comparison with other, nonutilitarian consequentialist theories.

Jeremy Bentham and the Hedonistic Calculus

Reforming the System of Justice

- The Age of Enlightenment is introduced, and the general historical background for Bentham's project is given.
- The theory that happiness is intrinsically valuable.

The Hedonistic Calculus

- Bentham's seven steps in the hedonistic calculus.
- Criticism of Bentham's calculus: The values are arbitrary and biased.

SUGGESTION

Because the hedonistic calculus presents a subject that the students can work with in a hands-on fashion, you may want to ask the class for a suggestion of a moral dilemma: two mutually exclusive courses of action they may have to choose between. Usually, the dilemma of deciding to leave school and find work versus staying in school to get a degree works very well. On the board you may clearly demonstrate not only how the calculus works but also that the values assigned to each factor are biased, based on the preferences we already have for a certain result.

The Uncertain Future

- It is difficult to make a utilitarian choice when you don't know the exact outcome of your intended action.
- J. S. Mill's answer to criticism of utilitarianism.

The Moral Universe of Utilitarianism: Advantages and Problems of Sheer Numbers

- The capacity for suffering makes one a member of the moral universe.
- What creates happiness or decreases unhappiness for the majority is morally right by definition.
- Moral problems in utilitarianism: Can a minority be sacrificed for the sake of the majority? And if so, under what circumstances?

John Stuart Mill: Higher and Lower Pleasures

Some Pleasures Are Higher Than Others

- J. S. Mill's background and his attempt to redesign utilitarianism.
- The distinction between higher and lower pleasures, and the test for identification of the higher pleasures.

The students may understand the distinction between higher and lower pleasures better if you give them several different examples—not just the choice between watching a sitcom or watching PBS, but also the different joys of an easily obtainable pleasure (such as having a beer, or whatever) versus a pleasure that is harder to achieve (such as finally understanding a mathematical problem). You may also discuss with your class whether the pleasures that are harder to obtain are always preferable to the easier ones.

- Criticism of Mill's test: It is biased in favor of intellectual pleasures.

Mill's Political Vision: Equality and No Harm to Others

- In defense of Mill: He wished to educate the general population in order to make more options available to everybody.
- The harm principle: The only legitimate reason for interference with people is if they do harm to others.

The harm principle may provide for a good discussion, since it is a more liberal principle than the one the legislation of the United States is based on: Would the students approve of a principle that doesn't allow interference if a person does no harm to others, but only to himself or herself? You may want to include in the discussion the concept of indirectly influencing/indirectly harming another person.

- Limitations to the harm principle, including Mill's leaning toward cultural paternalism.

Act and Rule Utilitarianism

- The classical principle of utility versus the formulation of rule utilitarianism.
- Evaluation of rule utilitarianism.
- Reference to Chapter 7 and story outlines concerning utilitarianism versus deontology: "The Blacksmith and the Baker," *The Brothers Karamazov*, "The Ones Who Walk Away from Omelas," *Abandon Ship!*, *High Noon*, *Rebel Without a Cause*, and *Star Trek: The Next Generation*: "Justice."

Boxes

Intrinsic Versus Instrumental Values   Introduces the concept of value in itself and value leading to another value.

The Naturalistic Fallacy   Discusses the problem inherent in Mill's argument that happiness is desirable because it is desired: moving from an "is" to an "ought."

SUGGESTION ————————————————————————————

You may wish to refer your students to Chapters 15 and 18 where the naturalistic fallacy is further discussed.

Mill and the Women's Cause   Mill's fight for equal rights, inspired by Harriet Taylor.

Chapter 6: Using Your Reason, Part 2: Kant's Deontology

This chapter introduces Kant's deontology with the main focus on (1) the good will and the categorical imperative and (2) the theory of rational beings as ends in themselves. The issue of absolutism (hard universalism) is discussed, as is the topic of autonomy. (The question of nonrational beings is taken up in Chapter 14.)

Main Points

- Definition of *deontology:* duty theory.

To Do the Right Thing
The Good Will

- What counts morally is not the assurance of good consequences, but the presence of a good will.

The Categorical Imperative

- Introduction to the categorical imperative, and to Immanuel Kant as a hard universalist.
- The example of the shopkeeper: hypothetical versus categorical imperative.

SUGGESTION ————————————————————————————

Here you may want to discuss whether (as Kant would suggest) a person who likes to help is morally inferior to one who doesn't but who helps anyway as a matter of principle. In Chapter 11 there is a discussion of this subject: Philippa Foot argues that the person who likes to help is morally superior to the other.

- Kant's example of the man who wants to borrow money and who uses the categorical imperative to dissuade himself.
- Humans as autonomous lawmakers.

Kant's Critics

- J. S. Mill: Kant is referring to consequences.
- The categorical imperative cannot solve a conflict between two duties.
- The categorical imperative allows for a loophole: describing a situation so specifically that it cannot be universalized.
- The concept of "rational" may be ambiguous.

SUGGESTION

Redefining the concept of rationality: I have not included the following information in the chapter, because I thought it might sidetrack the discussion, but you may consider including it in your class material. There is a current debate about the definition of rationality and gender; according to some feminists, the traditional definition of rationality as defining one's goal and selecting the shortest route to accomplish it is a predominantly male viewpoint. Female rational behavior, they say, is rather an extensive information-gathering process that might demand a detour to the chosen goal or a redefinition of the goal. The consequences of this rethinking of the concept of rationality are intriguing. For one thing, it would cause many traditionalists to exclaim, "That's what I've said all along! Women are irrational and can't make up their minds!" Although many men and women might approve of an expanded definition of rationality, many women might not like the implication, thought to be long abandoned, that their logic is somehow faulty or of a different nature than men's—or that if they think rationally in the traditional sense, they are somehow less feminine. Although the question of a redefinition of rationality is fascinating, it is as explosive as other questions of human nature when applied to gender issues.

- The categorical imperative allows for no exceptions.

Rational Beings Are Ends in Themselves
Never as Means to an End Only

- Definition of means to an end versus end in oneself.

SUGGESTION

In order to facilitate understanding, you may want to have students come up with suggestions as to what it is to treat someone as a means to an end only, and point out that there is a difference between mutual, respectful use, and unilateral abuse. It is usually harder for students to understand what an "end in oneself" is, so the contrast to "merely a means to an end" is useful.

- The egalitarian aspect of Kant's principle.
- Rational beings are priceless value-givers and should be treated with respect.
- One should not treat oneself as a means to an end, either.
- The difference between treating someone as a "means to an end" and as "merely a means to an end."

Beings Who Are Things

- The expansion of the moral universe to cover all rational beings.
- The problem with nonrational beings: Are animals and some categories of humans to be classified as "things"?

SUGGESTION _____

If your syllabus includes Chapter 14, you may want to save the debate about the abuse of animals until then. If not, you may want to discuss the subject here: Are animals nonrational? And, if they are, does it mean we can treat them like things? You may want to refer your students to Chapter 14.

- The kingdom of ends: The combination of the categorical imperative and the principle of not treating people as means may soften the hard universalist principle of the categorical imperative.
- Reference to Chapter 7 and story outlines exploring the theories of utilitarianism versus deontology: "The Blacksmith and the Baker," *The Brothers Karamazov*, "The Ones Who Walk Away from Omelas," *Abandon Ship!*, *High Noon*, *Rebel Without a Cause*, and *Star Trek: The Next Generation*: "Justice."

Box

Kant: His Life and Work   Introduces Immanuel Kant and his principal works.

Chapter 7: Narratives of Right and Wrong Conduct

This chapter provides the narrative discussion material for Chapters 3–6, and each story outlined has several study questions following it. The subjects of cultural diversity and ethical relativism are illustrated in the films *Do the Right Thing* and *The Last of the Mohicans*, the novel *A Passage to India*, the film *Lawrence of Arabia*, and the science fiction novel *Sideshow*. Egoism is illustrated in the novels *Madame Bovary*, *Gone with the Wind*, and *Atlas Shrugged*. Utilitarianism and Kantian deontology are discussed and contrasted in the satirical poem "The Blacksmith and the Baker," the novel *The Brothers Karamazov*, the short story "The Ones Who Walk Away from Omelas," and the films *Abandon Ship!*, *Rebel Without a Cause*, and *High Noon*, and the television episode "Justice" from *Star Trek: The Next Generation*.

Main Points

Dealing with Differences

- This section provides material for Chapter 3, Ethical Relativism. The first four story outlines deal with the aspect of cultural tolerance and diversity as a positive thing; the final one is a direct criticism of ethical relativism taken to the extreme.
- The film *Do the Right Thing* (1989) illustrates the issue of racial and cultural diversity in a neighborhood. In a predominantly black neighborhood, an Italian pizza restaurant is the focus of attention, and later of violence.
- The film *The Last of the Mohicans* (1992), based on the James Fenimore Cooper novel, provides a historical view of cultural lack of understanding. Taking place in prerevolution America, it tells about the culture clashes between Europeans and native tribes.
- *A Passage to India*, the novel (1924) and the film (1984), tells about the misunderstandings between a young British woman and an Indian doctor in early twentieth-century India.
- *Lawrence of Arabia* (1962), the film about the real-life story of T. H. Lawrence and his fight for Arab independence, tells about the communication problems and successes between Lawrence and his Arab friends.
- A direct criticism of the noninterference policy of ethical relativism is provided by an excerpt from the novel *Sideshow* (1992), where the planet Elsewhere is a model for strictly enforced cultural diversity.

SOME ADDITIONAL NARRATIVES ILLUSTRATING THE THEME OF CULTURAL DIVERSITY

William Shakespeare, *The Merchant of Venice, play (1600).*

Ralph Ellison, *Invisible Man,* novel (1947).

Doris Lessing, *The Grass Is Singing,* novel (1950).

Hester Street, film (1975).

M. M. Kaye, *The Far Pavillions,* novel (1978). Has been made into a fairly good television miniseries, but I suggest not using the two-hour video version. It is too abbreviated to make any sense whatsoever.

Moscow on the Hudson, film (1984).

My Beautiful Laundrette, film (1985).

A Stranger Among Us, film (1992).

Thunderheart, film (1992).

Michael Crichton, *Rising Sun,* novel and film (1993).

Egoism

- This section provides discussion material for Chapter 4, Myself or Others?
- *Madame Bovary* (novel, 1857; films, 1949 and 1991) is the story of a young woman who is bored with her provincial life and selfishly sets out to entertain herself.
- *Gone with the Wind* (novel, 1937; film, 1939) tells of the strong will and ruthless pursuit of purpose of Scarlett O'Hara in the South of the Civil War and the years following the war.
- *Atlas Shrugged* (novel, 1957) is represented with a lengthy excerpt illustrating ethical egoism in Ayn Rand's version: To let yourself be abused by parasites is morally wrong.

SUGGESTION

After completing *The Moral of the Story* I had the opportunity to see the 1992 film *Hero,* and I recommend this film as an intelligent exploration of the topic of egoism versus altruism: Is it possible for a generally selfish person to act heroically on occasion, and might we all have the capability to act selflessly when the situation calls for it? The film is funny and poignant, with a conclusion reminiscent of the classic films of Frank Capra, presenting a moral problem of its own: Is it morally acceptable to perpetuate a lie if it inspires people to do the right thing?

SOME ADDITIONAL NARRATIVES ILLUSTRATING THE THEME OF EGOISM

Honoré de Balzac, *Père Goriot,* novel (1834).

Rudyard Kipling, "The Man Who Would Be King," short story (1888–1890). Made into an excellent film (1975).

Nightmare Alley, film (1947).

Rashomon, film (1950).

The Blue Max, film (1966).

Save the Tiger, film (1973).

Wall Street, film (1987).

The Story of Women, film (1988).

Pretty Woman, film (1990).

SOME NARRATIVES ILLUSTRATING
THE THEME OF ALTRUISM/SELF-SACRIFICE

There is no narrative selection of stories covering the topic of altruism in *The Moral of the Story*, but I would like to list a number of stories that might be used to illustrate the subject:

"Faithful John," *Grimm's Fairy Tales*, short story (1812–1815).

Charles Dickens, *A Tale of Two Cities*, novel (1859), film (1935, 1958).

Henrik Ibsen, *The Wild Duck*, play (1884).

Ernest Hemingway, *For Whom the Bell Tolls*, novel (1940), film (1943).

Casablanca, film (1942).

This Land Is Mine, film (1943).

Titanic, film (1953). May also be used to illustrate egoism!

The Alamo, film (1961). Use letterbox Director's Cut from 1992, restoring important missing scenes.

The Sacrifice, film (Swedish), 1986.

Glory, film (1989).

The Abyss, film (1989). As an illustration of altruism, use only the Director's Cut from 1993; in the 1989 version important sequences have been cut.

Hero, film (1992).

Utilitarianism and Deontology

- This section contains illustrations of both Chapter 5 and Chapter 6, since a criticism of one theme often implies a support for the other.

- Utilitarianism is criticized for its lack of concern for human rights in the story of "The Blacksmith and the Baker," a satirical poem (1777). A blacksmith is convicted of murder, but because the town cannot afford to lose its blacksmith, the townspeople execute one of their two bakers instead.

- In an excerpt from the novel *The Brothers Karamazov* (1881), the question is asked, Could one wish for a community's happiness to be based on the suffering of a child?

- "The Ones Who Walk Away from Omelas," a short story (1973), elaborates on the Dostoyevsky theme and tells a story of such a community whose happiness is bought at the price of a child's suffering. In essence it criticizes the basic value of utilitarianism.

- The film *Abandon Ship!* (1957) is based on a real-life story about a shipwreck: The captain has to put some lifeboat passengers overboard in order to save the lives of the rest. Here utilitarianism is evoked as the only solution to a real-life problem. *Abandon Ship!* can also be taken as an illustration of the universalization principle of the categorical imperative.

30

- *Rebel Without a Cause*, film (1955), is a story about the generation gap: The son is in trouble, and needs advice and support from his father. The film contains a generational debate between utilitarianism and deontology: The father represents calculating utilitarianism, while the son represents the search for absolute rightness.

- In the film *High Noon* (1952) a marshal of a small western town has to face avenging outlaws on the day of his wedding. It illustrates the principle of the categorical imperative: doing one's duty for the sake of the moral law in itself.

- In *Star Trek: The Next Generation*: "Justice," a young officer of Starfleet faces execution for a minor offense on an absolutist planet. This episode criticizes an absolutist principle for not allowing for exceptions.

SOME ADDITIONAL NARRATIVES ILLUSTRATING THE THEMES OF UTILITARIANISM AND DEONTOLOGY

PRIMARILY UTILITARIAN

Soylent Green, film (1973).

Rollerball, film (1975).

The Dead Zone, film (1983).

The Running Man, film (1987).

Roger McBride Allen, *Orphan of Creation*, novel (1988). See Chapter 20 for an outline of this novel used as an example of the issue of personhood.

Indecent Proposal, film (1992).

PRIMARILY DEONTOLOGICAL

Honoré de Balzac, *Père Goriot* (1834).

Henrik Ibsen, *Ghosts*, play (1881).

The Four Feathers, film (1939 [best], 1977).

Mr. Smith Goes to Washington, film (1939).

Fort Apache, film (1948).

Twelve O'Clock High, film (1949).

Prince of Foxes, film (1951). Machiavelianism versus deontology.

Shane, film (1952).

The Last Command, film (1955).

The Alamo, film (1961). Use letterbox Director's Cut from 1992, restoring important missing scenes.

The Conversation, film (1974).

Outland, film (1981).

The Last Starfighter, film (1984).

Gardens of Stone, film (1987).

Part 3: How Should I Be? Theories of Virtue

Part 3 examines the most influential theories of virtue in ancient and modern times.

Chapter 8: Socrates, Plato, and the Good Life

This chapter introduces the question of virtue ethics as an alternative or a supplement to theories of conduct, and discusses the concept of character. Next we look at Socrates's life and teachings and place him in a context of virtue ethics. Plato's role in ethics is examined, and his theory of forms is outlined.

Main Points

Virtue Ethics

What Is Virtue?

- Introduces virtue ethics and the question of developing a good character (how should I be) versus ethics of conduct (what should I do?).

What Is Character?

- Discusses whether character is something you are born with and cannot change or whether character can be molded.

SUGGESTION

Your students may enjoy discussing whether character is something one is born with or whether it can be changed. You may want to point out that this is a false dichotomy: One may be born with character potential, but this has to be molded.

The Case for Virtue Ethics

- The decline of virtue ethics and the rise of ethics of conduct. Arguments in favor of a return to virtue ethics.

The Question of How to Live

The Good Teacher

- The teacher–student relationship between Socrates and Plato.
- Socrates: "The unexamined life is not worth living."

Socrates, Man of Athens

- The dialectic (Socratic) method.
- The life of Socrates as a man of the polis.

The Death of Socrates and the Works of Plato

- The trial and death of Socrates.
- Plato's reaction; Plato's *Dialogues.*

The Good Life

- The difference between opinion and true knowledge.
- Socrates's fight against relativism.
- Socrates's concept of virtue and truth-seeking.

The Virtuous Person

- The answer to Glaucon in *The Republic:* A virtuous person is in balance.
- The three parts of the psyche: reason, spirit, and desires. (This theory is also explored in Chapter 18.)

The Forms and the Good

What Is a Form?

- Introduces the concept of metaphysics: theories about the nature of reality.
- Defines the theory of Forms. Example: the Form of Bed. Asks whether there are Forms for negatives.

The Form of the Good

- A hierarchy of Forms is presented.

SUGGESTION

Beginners in philosophy have difficulty understanding the theory of Forms. I have had some success approaching the subject by explaining that at Plato's time the Greek intellectuals did not think in terms of *concepts* of language, as we might, but of *entities;* in the mythological period it was customary to deify concepts, as in the case of the goddess Nike (Victory). Plato's form of the Good can be seen as a nontheological version of the same phenomenon.

- The theory of forms is illustrated by Plato's "Myth of the Cave."

SUGGESTION

If your students are receptive, you may want to introduce them to the "third man" problem; I did not include it in the text because I found that it took the reader too far from the general topic of virtue. The "third man" criticizes Plato's Forms for ending in an infinite regress of Forms. It assumes that Plato's theory of Forms rests on the assumption that the Forms are *like* their copies in the tangible world. The Form of Beauty is beautiful, the Form of a puppy looks like a generic puppy. You may try an example along these lines (the "third man" is usually grasped easily only by a few students in a lower-division class): If two cats are both identified as cats, Plato would say, it is because they both participate in the Form Cat, in "catness," so to speak. So, in order to compare two things (like two cats), we need a third thing (a "third man," like the Form Cat) to compare them with. But how can we tell that one cat (cat_1) and the Form Cat (Cat_2) are alike? There must be some higher Form of Cat (Cat_3) with which we compare cat_1 and Cat_2. And how do we know that Cat_3 is like cat_1 and Cat_2?

(continued)

34

There must be an even higher Form, Cat$_4$, that serves as a basis of comparison, and so forth. You may want to mention to your students that Aristotle considered this such a serious blow to the theory of Forms that he, himself, abandoned the Platonic idea that Forms are separate from things and held that there are Forms, but they are embedded in the world of things, existing as the cause that makes things retain their shape and identity (the formal cause). Aristotle's theory of causes will be mentioned in Chapter 9.

- The Platonic legacy in Christianity.

Boxes

Victims of Fanaticism   The murder of Hypatia, and the burning of the library at Alexandria.

Three Theories of Metaphysics   Introduces the concepts of Materialism, Idealism, and Dualism.

The Theory of Anamnesis   Presents Plato's theory of anamnesis and connects it with the concept of reincarnation.

The Cave   A short presentation of Plato's "Myth of the Cave": The prisoners who see shapes on the wall, believing them to be reality.

Chapter 9: Aristotle's Virtue Theory

The extent of Aristotle's role in philosophy is outlined, including his concept of teleology and causation. In particular his theory of virtue is examined with examples. The chapter concludes with an overall discussion of virtue theory.

Main Points

Aristotle the Scientist

Empirical Knowledge and the Realm of the Senses

- Aristotle's life and influence as a philosopher and a scientist.

Life, the Universe, and Everything

- The importance of logic and observation for Aristotle; his intellectual interests in metaphysics, politics, drama, rhetoric, and so on.

Teleology: The Concept of Purpose

- Aristotle's theory that everything has a purpose.

Aristotle and the Virtues

Virtue and Excellence

- For Aristotle "virtue" means doing something with excellence.

Is There a Human Purpose?

- The telos for humans as a species, and the telos for an individual person, are both defined by that species's or person's potential.
- The human purpose is to use one's reason well.
- Aristotle's two forms of virtue: intellectual and moral.

The Virtues

- The Golden Mean: not too much, and not too little.

SUGGESTION

You may want to relate this theory to everyday experiences. Aristotle believes it is virtuous to know when an effort is sufficient; you may want to ask your students for examples from personal experience (such as putting the right amount of effort into studying for an exam or writing a term paper). Also, the question of "what is the right amount" is something most people have to face continually: How grateful should I be? How friendly should I be? How assertive should I be? The question of gratitude is explored further in Chapter 12.

- Discussion of three questions about Aristotle's virtue theory: (1) If this is supposed to be a theory of character, why does Aristotle talk about conduct? (2) What does developing a good character have to do with rational thinking? (3) Are we supposed to do *everything* in the right amount, such as stealing and lying?
- The Golden Mean is relative to the situation.
- Discussion of examples of Aristotle's virtues: courage, temperance, pride, being even-tempered, truthfulness, wit.

SUGGESTION

Your students may enjoy finding additional examples of the general pattern of vice-virtue-vice. A board diagram is useful, lining all vices of deficiency up on one side, virtues in the middle, and vices of excess on the other side.

- Two dispositions of vice, with virtue in the middle. How does one find the virtue? By trial and error, and developing good habits.

Happiness

- Aristotle's idea of well-being: contemplation.
- The death of Aristotle, and the fate of his school and his ideas.

Some Objections to Greek Virtue Theory

- The advantage of ethics of conduct over virtue ethics: recourse to a common law.
- Virtue ethics is based in teleology, and we cannot make assumptions about natural human purposes.
- Reference to Chapter 13 and outlines of stories concerning virtues and vices that Aristotle might have recognized.

Boxes

The Four Causes   Aristotle's theory of causation: material, efficient, formal, and final causes.

Teleological Explanations   Discusses a teleological type of explanation versus a causal explanation.

Is There a Human Purpose?   Two other thinkers reflecting on the theme of human purpose: Saint Thomas Aquinas and Jean-Paul Sartre.

The Right Decision at the Right Time   Example of Aristotle's virtue theory: three women on a bridge watching a child being swept downriver. One is cowardly, one is rash, and one is courageous.

The Clash Between Classical and Christian Virtues   A comparison between Aristotle's list of virtues and the traditional Christian list of cardinal virtues and cardinal sins.

Chapter 10: Virtues and Values of Other Traditions

This chapter provides an introduction to a selection of moral viewpoints rarely discussed in Western ethics courses of the past. The viewpoints selected are the ethics of Confucius and Mencius; Buddhism; Islam; the Judaic tradition; the moral views of the Vikings; African virtue theory; and Native American value theory.

Main Points

Asian Traditions

Confucius and Mencius

- Confucius's theory of a man of virtue: someone who is wise, courageous, and humane, and who strives to develop good habits and continual good thinking.
- Mencius's theory that humans are born morally good and lose their goodness through bad influence. Development of one's character and recapturing one's lost goodness is virtuous.

A discussion of whether humans are born good or not would be appropriate here. You may want to refer your students to Chapter 17, which discusses the subject in greater detail.

- Mencius quote: Taking care of one's parents and developing one's character are moral duties.

Buddhism

- The life of Siddhartha Gautama.
- The concept of enlightenment and the Four Noble Truths: (1) life is suffering, (2) suffering is caused by craving for life, (3) if craving ceases, suffering will cease, and (4) the way to stop craving is to follow the Noble Eightfold Path.

Other Traditions

Islam

- A brief history of Islam.
- A description of some of the most important doctrines of Islam: the view of reality, free will, and the sin of disobedience.

Judaism

- The philosophy of Moses Maimonides: the importance of wisdom, and the doctrine of the four levels of perfection.
- The tradition of charity and compassion.

The Virtues of the Vikings

- The Viking tradition of justice among equals, loyalty to family and friends, honor in battle, and trusting in one's good luck.

African Virtue Theory

- The virtue ethics of the Akan people in West Africa: A good character is acquired through good habits.
- Virtues are taught through storytelling, habituating the children to moral virtues.

Native American Values and the Environment

- The association of Native American values and ecological virtue is evaluated: a true connection or an ideal?

- Reference to Chapter 13 and story outlines illustrating virtues and vices incorporating non-Western/noncontemporary values: *Njal's Saga*, *The Seven Samurai*, *Ivanhoe*, "The Warrior Maiden."

Boxes

Confucius and Aristotle   Discusses the similarities and differences between Confucius and Aristotle.

Taoism   A short introduction to the philosophy of Lao-Tzu, the concept of the Way, and the opposing forces of Yin and Yang.

Karma   The Hindu doctrine of karma and reincarnation is explored and compared with its Buddhist development. (Karma will also be discussed in Chapter 15.)

Islam and the Protection of Women   An evaluation of the traditional Islamic rules restricting women's rights.

Maimonides and the Death Penalty   The range of crimes punishable by death according to Maimonides.

Rules of Viking Life   A selection of virtues listed in the Icelandic epic poem Havamal. The most famous one: "Cattle die, kindred die, you yourself will die. What never dies is the good name you have won for yourself."

Chapter 11: The Modern Perspective

This chapter looks at modern virtue theory, first in the new American tradition represented by the philosophers Bernard Mayo, Philippa Foot, and Christina Hoff Sommers, and second, within the modern continental tradition of the quest for authenticity. The philosophers represented here are Søren Kierkegaard, Martin Heidegger, and Jean-Paul Sartre.

Main Points

A Revival of Virtue Theory

Explores some strengths and weaknesses of virtue ethics, and the difference between a morality of virtue and an ethics of virtue. ("Morality" moralizes, and "ethics" questions.)

Have Virtue, and Then Go Ahead

Bernard Mayo

- Mayo: If we have a set of virtues, we usually choose the right conduct; however, ethics of conduct does not guarantee that one becomes a good person, only that one does right.
- Exemplars should be emulated.

Philippa Foot

- Foot: Virtues are not merely dispositions that we cannot be held accountable for, but a matter of intention—a good will to correct a tendency to go astray.
- Are naturally virtuous people as morally praiseworthy as people who make an effort to overcome a bad inclination? Foot claims that naturally virtuous people are morally superior.

SUGGESTION

If you didn't have this discussion in the Kant section, you may want to discuss with your students at this point whether a morally superior person is one who is able to conquer her own bad inclinations or one who has no bad inclinations to conquer.

Christina Hoff Sommers

- Sommers's argument for teaching virtues in classrooms in order to avoid the spread of ethical subjectivism.
- There are moral values that cannot be disputed, such as "to think only of yourself, to steal, to lie, to break promises."
- Sommers's call to a strengthening of moral values is evaluated and criticized, because an element is missing: arguments in support of virtues based on reason.

The Quest for Authenticity

- The virtue of authenticity in the philosophy of existentialism.

Kierkegaard

- The life and influence of Søren Kierkegaard, and his emotional ties to his father.
- Kierkegaard's quote from *Stages on Life's Way* concerning his father.
- The feeling of *angst* (anguish, dread) at having to make choices.
- The concept of the subjectivity of truth: Only the individual can reach what is the truth for him or her. It cannot be adopted from someone else.
- The theory of the three stages in life: the aesthetic stage, the ethical stage, and the religious stage, reached by a leap of faith.

Heidegger's Intellectual Authenticity

- Martin Heidegger's theory of human existence as a fundamental interaction with the world. The term for humans: "Being-There" (*Dasein*).

- The inauthentic situations for humans happen when they let themselves believe that they are merely things affected by circumstances. Authenticity is gained when humans take responsibility, choose to think for themselves, and realize they can interact with the world and affect it.
- Heidegger's concept of anguish: the realization that all human concerns and rules are relative and that there is no absolute truth.
- Evaluation of Heidegger's concept of authenticity: merely a call to reexamine ourselves ("getting in touch with ourselves") or a constant state of intellectual open-mindedness?

Sartre's Ethical Authenticity

- A presentation of Jean-Paul Sartre's role in the existential movement.
- Because there are no objective values, according to existentialism, life is absurd. This means that humans can create their own values through the process of choice, and only through choosing can one attain authenticity.
- Anguish is felt at the moment of choice and may lead to the inauthenticity of deluding oneself that one does not have to choose because one has no options. This is known as "bad faith."
- Example of bad faith: the young woman on a date who thinks she can avoid choosing whether or not she wants a physical relationship with her date.
- Humans cannot avoid choosing: We are condemned to be free.

SUGGESTION

At this point you may consider discussing whether or not the continental concern for authenticity qualifies as an example of virtue ethics. An argument in favor would be that Anglo-American virtue ethics is concerned with building up a good character, and integrity and responsibility (authenticity) can also be considered important elements of a good character. An argument against accepting theories of moral authenticity as part of a general virtue theory would focus on the issue of role models. Anglo-American virtue theory approves of role models as exemplars to follow, whereas the existentialist search for authenticity precludes merely following the example of other people: Emulating others could be seen as a way to avoid taking full responsibility for one's own life and situation—in other words, bad faith. It may interest your students to discuss whether one can be authentic and also have role models, and whether authenticity must necessarily imply acting without inspiration from others.

- Authenticity depends on your accomplishments, not on what you intended to do but never got done.

- The concept of ego integrity, coined by Erik Erikson. Psychologists recognize the concept of authenticity in resolving crisis situations. Persons with ego integrity take responsibility for their actions but don't agonize over things they have no control over.
- Reference to Chapter 13 and story outlines illustrating the concepts of anguish and authenticity: *No Exit, Hannah and Her Sisters*, "The Tail," *Babette's Feast, Star Wars*, and *The Good Apprentice*.

Boxes

Can We Change Our Spots? Discusses whether we are responsible for our character and dispositions; virtue ethics claims we can improve on our character.

Negative Role Models Virtue ethics often focuses on heroes and saints, but important moral lessons in virtue are also learned from negative role models; here are some examples of real and fictional characters who may serve as negative role models.

Kant and His Rejection of Role Models Kant rejects the idea of choosing people to emulate, for the psychological reason that humans often tend to resent those they cannot measure up against. Typical situation: parents holding one child up as a model for the other child.

SUGGESTION

The boxes on negative role models and Kant's view on role models may serve as an exceptionally good topic for a class discussion: Are proponents of virtue ethics right when they claim that we can learn more easily from positive and negative role models than from rules of conduct, or is Kant right that being exposed to role models breeds resentment? You may want your students to evaluate whether they themselves generally learn most from positive role models, negative role models, or rules of conduct.

MacIntyre and the Virtues Alasdair MacIntyre's theory of the importance of cultural tradition in a value theory. (MacIntyre's virtue theory will be discussed further in Chapter 19.)

A Kind of Love and a Marriage That Wasn't: Regine Olsen The story of Kierkegaard's relationship with Regine Olsen, and his attempts to make her break off the engagement.

Heidegger and the Nazi Connection Heidegger's relationship to his teacher Edmund Husserl, and Heidegger's role during the Nazi reign in Germany.

Henri Bergson: Let Your True Self Emerge Bergson's theory of time and free will is briefly outlined. For Bergson, the experience of our true self happens as a break-through experience when we act in a way we had not expected ourselves to act. The deeper self emerges in spite of customs and reason. Bergson's life and death are briefly described.

Chapter 12: Case Studies in Virtue

Here two virtues are selected to be examined in detail: compassion and gratitude. Philip Hallie's account of compassion shown by a French village during World War II is presented, and Richard Taylor's view that compassion is the only virtue needed is critically examined. Next, the Chinese tradition of gratitude toward one's parents (Lin Yutang) is contrasted with Jane English's criticism of the debt-metaphor ("We owe our parents nothing"), and the concept of friendship duties is examined.

Main Points

Compassion: Are We Born with It?

- In contrast to Thomas Hobbes, David Hume and Jean-Jacques Rousseau agree that humans are born with compassion toward others. For Rousseau it is civilization that corrupts the original fellow-feeling. (Rousseau's philosophy will be discussed further in Chapter 17.)

Philip Hallie: The Case of Le Chambon

- Hallie's account of the compassion shown by a French village toward Jewish refugees during World War II.
- The concept of institutionalized cruelty, and an analysis of why it happens and how it can be helped.

Richard Taylor: Compassion Is All You Need

- Taylor's three examples of atrocities: In common for all three are malice and lack of compassion. There is no need for reason in choosing compassion.
- Taylor's three compassionate examples. Same conclusion: We don't need reason in order to be compassionate.
- Criticism of Taylor: If some humans have no compassion, reason must be used to persuade them.
- The story *Huckleberry Finn* is used as an example of how compassion may be sufficient sometimes, but not at other times when rational judgment is needed.

SUGGESTION

It is likely that some of your students don't know the story of Huck Finn, especially if you have many exchange students or immigrant students in your class. Since it is a controversial story to some because of its use of typical nineteenth-century language which today is identified as racist, you may want to
(continued)

---

summarize the story and spend a few minutes discussing if it is fair to criticize *Huckleberry Finn* for being a racist piece of literature. You may want to point your students' attention to the caption of the drawing of Huck and Jim: The character of Huck may have been based on an African-American boy.

Gratitude: How Much, and When?

- There is a difference between feeling gratitude and showing gratitude. We can't be forced to feel something we don't feel, but we can make a show of gratitude when it is appropriate.

We Owe Our Parents Everything

- The Chinese philosopher Lin Yutang expresses the Chinese traditional belief that age deserves respect.
- According to Lin Yutang, we owe a debt of gratitude to our parents for having raised us.
- Conditions in modern China with its restrictions on childbirth and its socialized care of the elderly.

SUGGESTION

Here you may want to discuss with your students the traditions of the East and the West in terms of attitude toward the elderly; some of your students may be of Latino or of some other ethnic, Western background that actively values the elderly of a community, and it is likely that they may want to point out that a caring traditional attitude toward the elderly is not an exclusively Eastern way.

We Owe Our Parents Nothing

- Jane English claims that filial love is undermined if parents insist that their grown children are indebted to them.
- Appropriate and inappropriate ways of using the "debt-metaphor." Debts require reciprocation, whereas friendship duties are mutual and are not defined by past favors.
- Obligations based on love and friendship depend on (1) the need of the parents and (2) the ability and resources of the grown child.

Friendship Duties and Gratitude

- Fred Berger's answer to questions of the extent of gratitude one ought to show: Unsolicited favors need not be reciprocated; however, if they are done for the recipient's own sake, the recipient is treated as an end in himself or herself in the

Kantian sense, and gratitude is owed. If favors are done for the sake of the giver (treating the recipient as a means to an end), no gratitude is owed.

- How much gratitude should we show? The Aristotelian "right amount," varying from case to case.

Virtue and Conduct: Ethical Pluralism?

- An evaluation of ethical pluralism as an example of soft universalism in practice: allowing for a multitude of moral approaches, while seeking common agreement on some basic underlying values.
- Reference to Chapter 13 and story outlines concerning the virtues of compassion and gratitude: "The Good Samaritan" and *Ivanhoe*.

Boxes

Is It Better to Cry Over Your Victim Than Not to Feel Sorry? Jonathan Bennett's claim that it is better to have compassion even if you cause death and destruction than not to have compassion at all, is contrasted to Hallie's criticism, using an example from *Alice in Wonderland:* the Walrus and the Carpenter eating oysters.

Carol Gilligan: Compassion Is What Men Need Discusses the theory of psychologist Carol Gilligan that boys and men have a natural tendency to look to concepts of right and justice, whereas girls and women tend to be more inclined toward care and compassion. (Gilligan's theory will be discussed further in Chapter 16.)

Reason and Feeling A variety of views on whether morality and feelings are related. An example of a fictional group of people who are unemotional but who have a strong sense of ethics.

Love as a Virtue Discusses whether people can actually keep promises to love one another. Suggests that we don't promise to feel passion, but to show loyalty and caring.

What About Relatives? English's theory of friendship duties does not cover the situation of distant relatives in need of help.

Self-Worth and Retirement The Western attitude of self-worth being connected with one's usefulness and productivity is discussed.

Does the Golden Rule Always Work? Discussion of cases where applying the Golden Rule does not work, such as in the example by Deborah Tannen.

Dating, Debt, and Friendship English analyzes the dating situation and finds that a woman does not owe a man any favors if he takes her out as a gesture of friendship. This situation is further discussed.

Chapter 13: Narratives of Virtue and Vice

Structured similarly to Chapter 7, this chapter provides discussion material for Chapters 9 through 12 (there are no stories in this chapter directly associated with Plato's theory of virtue). I have chosen stories that in some way explore the virtues and vices that usually concern virtue ethics rather than stories that speak for or against virtue ethics as such. Three traditional virtues are selected: courage, honor, and compassion. Stories illustrating these virtues are chosen partially from a cross-cultural perspective; courage is represented by the novel *Lord Jim* and the Icelandic epic *Njal's Saga*. Honor is represented by the film *The Seven Samurai*. Next, two "vices we love" are examined: jealousy, in the play of *Othello*, the story "The Warrior Maiden," and the film *Fatal Attraction;* and thirst for revenge, in the novels *The Count of Monte Cristo* and *Moby Dick* and the film *The Searchers*.

Next, a selection of stories depict virtue theory in a modern perspective by focusing on (1) the feeling of Angst: the play *No Exit*, the film *Hannah and Her Sisters*, and the short story "The Tail"; and (2) the quest for authenticity: the novelette and film *Babette's Feast*, the film *Star Wars*, and the novel *The Good Apprentice*.

Main Points

Some Traditional Virtues

Courage

- In Joseph Conrad's novel *Lord Jim* (1900, film 1965), a young officer in the British Mercantile Marine believes himself to be destined for heroic deeds, but when the time for testing comes, he succumbs to his fear of death and abandons ship during a storm, leaving the passengers to fend for themselves. For the rest of his life he engages in acts of bravery to atone for his act of cowardice.
- In the Icelandic epic of *Njal's Saga* (ca. 1280 C.E.), Njal and his wife Bergthora with their grandchild are held prisoners in their farmhouse by their blood-feud enemies, and Bergthora and the child choose to face death with Njal rather than to accept the enemy's offer of safety.

SOME ADDITIONAL STORIES ILLUSTRATING
THE THEMES OF COURAGE AND COWARDICE

Hans Christian Andersen, "The Little Mermaid," fairy tale (1837).
The Lives of a Bengal Lancer, film (1935).

Ernest Hemingway, *For Whom the Bell Tolls*, novel (1940), film (1943).

This Land Is Mine, film (1943).

The Red Badge of Courage, film (1951).

The Bridge on the River Kwai, film (1957).

They Came to Cordura, film (1959).

633 Squadron, film (1964).

Khartoum, film (1966).

Seven Women, film (1966).

"Masada," television miniseries (1980).

A Love in Germany, film (1984).

Backdraft, film (1991).

Honor

- The Japanese film *The Seven Samurai* (1954) is the selected example of honor as a virtue, but it can also be used in conjunction with Chapter 10 on Asian virtues and values. A sixteenth-century Japanese village is being sacked repeatedly by bandits, and the villagers hire seven samurai warriors to defend the village against the upcoming assault. In the film we are introduced to the virtues of a Samurai warrior: He must be gentle, fearless, skillful, and modest, and he must understand loyalty and teamwork. Above all, he must live up to the Samurai standard of honor.

SOME ADDITIONAL STORIES ILLUSTRATING THE THEME OF HONOR

Edmond Rostand, *Cyrano de Bergerac*, novel (1897), film (1950, 1990).

Joseph Conrad, *Lord Jim*, novel (1900), film (1965).

The Four Feathers, film (1939), television film (1977).

Lawrence of Arabia, film (1962).

Heinrich Böll, *The Lost Honor of Katharina Blum*, novel (1974), film (1975).

The Duelists, film (1977).

The Story of Qui Ju, film (1993 U.S. release).

Compassion

- The parable of Jesus of Nazareth, "The Good Samaritan," is our first illustration of compassion. A man from Samaria is the only one helping a victim of mugging, even though others have passed him by. The impact of the story depends on the reader being aware that people from Samaria were thought of as outcasts by the Jewish contemporaries of Jesus.

- Sir Walter Scott's novel *Ivanhoe* (1820) is our other illustration of compassion; the section chosen is Ivanhoe's relationship with the Jew Isaac and his daughter

Rebecca. Ivanhoe, a son of a Saxon nobleman, is returning from the Crusades and helps an elderly Jew escape an ambush. The Jew, Isaac, later shows his gratitude by furnishing Ivanhoe with equipment to partake in a tournament, and when Ivanhoe is wounded, it is Isaac and Rebecca who nurse him back to life—not Ivanhoe's father, who has disowned him.

SOME ADDITIONAL STORIES ILLUSTRATING
THE THEME OF COMPASSION

"The Hut in the Forest," *Grimm's Fairy Tales*, short story (1812–15).

Hell in the Pacific, film (1968).

Barry B. Longyear, *Enemy Mine*, short story (1979), film (1985).

Awakenings, film (1990).

The Fisher King, film (1991).

City of Joy, film (1992).

Vices We Love

- This section relates directly to the box on negative role models in Chapter 11: Often we learn more about virtues from negative examples than from positive ones. Two classical vices are explored here, jealousy and thirst for revenge.

Jealousy

- William Shakespeare's *Othello* (1603–1604) shows the agony of the jealousy that has been planted in Othello's heart after it is maliciously and falsely suggested to him by Iago (himself jealous of Othello's success) that his wife, Desdemona, is having an affair with his friend Cassio. This accusation spells doom for everyone involved in the drama.

- The Pueblo Indian story of "The Warrior Maiden" is an example of jealousy. Red Hawk tries to break up Blue Hawk's perfect marriage by suggesting that Red Hawk's wife is unfaithful to him, and he sets out to prove it to Blue Hawk. By way of subterfuge he makes Blue Hawk believe him, and Blue Hawk puts his wife in a trunk, which he then throws in the river. She does not drown, however, but returns as a great warrior and exacts revenge on Red Hawk and forgives her husband.

- The film *Fatal Attraction* (1987) is our last example of jealousy. A woman becomes the lover of a married man, but after their brief affair she finds herself pregnant and demands a share in his life. Because he is not willing to give up his family for her, she proceeds to torment him and his family to the point of their destruction.

Thirst for Revenge

- This section begins with a brief analysis of the difference between revenge and retribution: Retribution is done by society, as a logical measure, whereas revenge (vengeance) is undertaken privately and may exceed the severity of the initial crime.

SUGGESTION

You may wish to bring up the question of capital punishment in this connection, and ask your students whether execution of a criminal is retribution or revenge. If your class has done a detailed study of utilitarianism and Kantianism, you may want to include these perspectives in the debate; for the utilitarian, capital punishment is permissible only if it accomplishes better consequences than imprisonment, in terms of deterrence or protection of the public. Rehabilitation may, for the utilitarian, have better overall consequences. For the Kantian, retribution is the only answer, because it asks the question whether the criminal is guilty or not, not what is better for society, and retribution ensures that the punishment fits the crime—in other words, that it does not exceed (or fall short of) the magnitude of the crime. For a Kantian, the utilitarian is using the criminal merely as a means to an end if he or she is being punished for the sake of a social effect and not primarily because of the crime he or she has committed. For the Kantian, punishing a criminal for the crime is, as some scholars have pointed out, actually treating the criminal with respect in assuming that he or she made a conscious decision to commit the crime.

- Alexandre Dumas's *The Count of Monte Cristo* (1844) is the ultimate vengeance narrative. Edmond Dantes, a young sailor about to marry the girl he loves and become captain of a ship, finds himself thrown in a dungeon with no trial on the day of his wedding, a victim of the jealousy and egoism of people he thought were his friends. Fourteen years later he escapes and seeks to destroy his victimizers through careful planning that, in the end, backfires.

- Herman Melville's *Moby Dick* (1851) is the story of the vengeance quest of Captain Ahab, who has lost a leg to the white whale Moby Dick. The hunt for the white whale is witnessed by the young sailor Ishmael, who is the narrator and the sole survivor of the doomed expedition. Ahab finds his whale with the loss of his own life, the ship, and the lives of all the crew save one.

- The last vengeance narrative is the film *The Searchers* (1956) about a civil war veteran, Ethan Edwards, searching for his only living relative, his niece, Debbie, who has been kidnapped by Comanche Indians after a raid that killed her family. After eight years Ethan finds his niece, but now he seeks to kill her since he considers her contaminated from living with the Indians.

SOME ADDITIONAL NARRATIVES ILLUSTRATING JEALOUSY, REVENGE, AND OTHER VICES

JEALOUSY

Leave Her to Heaven, film (1945).

Fay Weldon, *The Life and Loves of a She-Devil*, novel (1983). Never mind the 1989 film, but the British television series is interesting.

REVENGE

William Shakespeare, *Hamlet*, play (ca. 1600).

Fury, film (1936).

Son of Fury (1942). No relation to *Fury*!

Shadows of Forgotten Ancestors, film (1964).

High Plains Drifter, film (1973).

Death Wish, film (1974).

Star Trek II, The Wrath of Khan, film (1982).

Fay Weldon, *The Life and Loves of a She-Devil*, novel (1983).

Jean de Florette (part 1) and *Manon of the Spring* (part 2), films (1986).

Unforgiven, film (1992).

OBSESSION

Thomas Mann, "Death in Venice," short story (1911), film (1971).

The Offense, film (1973).

Tightrope, film (1984).

THE PRESENCE OF EVIL

Henry James, "The Turn of the Screw," short story (1898).

Strangers on a Train, film (1951).

The Bad Seed, film (1956).

In Cold Blood, film (1967).

BREAKING THE RULES

The Adventures of Don Juan, film (1948).

Tom Jones, film (1963).

Les Liaisons Dangereuses, play (1985) from story by Choderlos de Laclos; *Dangerous Liaisons*, film (1989).

Crimes and Misdemeanors, film (1989).

The Player, film (1992).

Virtue in a Modern Perspective: Angst and Authenticity

- Angst is of course not a virtue, or a vice, but facing up to one's feeling of anguish can be a virtue, and this is what some of the following stories illustrate.

Angst, Dread, Anguish, Anxiety, and So On

- Jean-Paul Sartre's play *No Exit* (1944) deals with three characters, a man and two women, doomed to spend an eternal afterlife in each other's company, each agonizing over the things they did in life, and worse, over the things they did not do.
- Woody Allen's film *Hannah and Her Sisters* (1986) illustrates the true existential angst of the hypochondriac: When the time comes he may actually have a fatal disease, he is paralyzed with fear. The fear turns to existential angst, however, when he learns that he is not ill after all. Instead of feeling relieved, he realizes that nothing is certain and that sooner or later he will die; now he truly faces the meaninglessness of life.
- The Swedish author Bertil Malmberg's short story "The Tail" tells of the little boy Åke who listens to a gruesome children's story about another little boy who becomes a monkey and is abandoned by everyone he loves, and now Åke believes that the same thing is happening to him.

SOME ADDITIONAL NARRATIVES ILLUSTRATING THE FEELING OF EXISTENTIAL ANGUISH AND THE ABSURDITY OF LIFE

Ernest Hemingway, *The Sun Also Rises*, novel (1926), film (1957, much better than the 1984 television version).

Franz Kafka, "The Metamorphosis," short story (1915); *The Trial*, novel (1935).

Albert Camus, *The Stranger*, novel (1942).

Samuel Beckett, *Waiting for Godot*, play (1954).

John Irving, *The World According to Garp*, novel (1978), film (1982).

Authenticity

The following titles explore the theme of being true to oneself, or seeking one's true identity: themes within the general category of ego integrity or authenticity.

- The novelette *Babette's Feast* (1953) and film (1988) by Karen Blixen (Isak Dinesen) tells of a Frenchwoman, a long-term refugee from the French Revolution, showing her gratitude to the two elderly sisters who took her in by spending her inheritance, treating them and their fundamentalist Christian congregation to a superb French dinner, and through this culinary masterpiece she regains her identity as a master-chef.

- The film *Star Wars* (1977), loved by a multitude of fans from children to the mythologist Joseph Campbell, tells of the beginning apprenticeship of Luke Skywalker as a Jedi Knight and of the Force that a knight can make use of. The Dark Side of the Force, however, is tempting, as it was to a former Jedi Knight, the formidable Darth Vader.

- Iris Murdoch's novel *The Good Apprentice* (1985) follows the agonies of Edward, who has caused his friend's death and can find no peace with himself, even if few others blame him. Through an inner journey Edward comes to grips with himself and his guilt.

SOME ADDITIONAL NARRATIVES ILLUSTRATING
AUTHENTICITY AND EGO INTEGRITY

Leo Tolstoi, *War and Peace*, novel (1864–69), film (1956, 1968).

Romain Rolland, *Jean Christophe*, novel (1905–12).

Thomas Hardy, *Far from the Madding Crowd*, novel (1912), film (1967).

Design for Living, film (1933).

Somerset Maugham, *The Razor's Edge*, novel (1943), film (1946); don't bother with the 1984 version).

The Man Who Shot Liberty Valence, film (1962).

Harry and Tonto, film (1974).

Local Hero, film (1983).

Children of a Lesser God, film (1986).

City Slickers, film (1991).

Leaving Normal, film (1992).

Thunderheart, film (1992).

Part 4: Ethics and Human Nature

Part 4 examines the most influential theories in Western tradition on human nature and places them in a context of ethical theory and practice.

Chapter 14: What Is a Person?

Here we ask the question "Who qualifies as a human being?" and distinguish between physical and moral criteria. Kant's theory of ends is reintroduced; the questions of animal rights and environmental ethics are brought up and connected with the concepts of rights and interests. Utilitarianism is reintroduced in the question of suffering as a moral criterion, and Kant's concept of rationality as a moral criterion is discussed.

Main Points

Introduction

- There is no present-day consensus on the precise definition of human nature; there are exclusive and inclusive definitions, and normative and descriptive definitions.

Who Qualifies as a Human Being?

SUGGESTION _____

Before your students read the chapter, you may consider having them list definitions of human nature and keep the list for reference and discussion material after studying Chapter 14. Were their definitions included in the book? Were they relevant? Try to have your students come up with a comprehensive theory of human nature incorporating elements from the text and their own viewpoint.

The Ethical Connection

- The connection between ethics and theories of human nature: Our definition of "human" determines how we treat those who qualify and those who don't.

The Issue of Physical Criteria?

- An overview of consequences of using physical criteria as determining factors.

The Person as a Moral Agent

- The concept of a person is introduced and defined as a moral agent.

The Expansion of the Concept "Human"

- A historical overview of how the concept of a person has expanded from a narrow definition to a broader one including humans of both genders and all races.

Kant Revisited: Humans Are Ends in Themselves

- Kant's theory of rational beings as ends in themselves is reintroduced, with a citation from *Grounding* (*Groundwork*), and criticized for containing problems for nonrational beings.

The Question of a Soul

Christians and Others

- The traditional Christian view: Humans have souls, animals do not.
- Comparison with views of other religions.

New Christians and Animal Rights

- Quote from a report by the World Council of Churches in 1988, including animals as creatures with integrity and value in themselves.

Rights and Personhood

Who Is a Person?

- Personhood as a normative concept; the extent of possible personhood, including nonhuman entities.
- Historical problems recognizing the personhood of women, children, slaves, and animals, and the question of rights and responsibilities in connection with the concept of personhood.

The Question of Interests and Rights

- The view of Joel Feinberg—whoever has interests should have rights—is discussed.

Suffering as a Moral Criterion

Human Suffering

- Reintroduction of Bentham's criterion for moral relevance: the capacity to suffer.
- How can we be certain that humans can suffer? Historical views on the subject.

Animal Suffering

- How can we be certain that animals can suffer? Historical views on the subject, including Descartes's: Animals cannot suffer.

SUGGESTION

Pet owners and other animal lovers among your students may enjoy discussing whether animals can feel pain and experience bonding. You are certain to get many examples of these phenomena from the class if you ask for them.

- Two counterarguments to Descartes: (1) Biology shows that humans and nonhuman animals are not very different, physiologically speaking, and (2) evolution would not have favored certain animal species if they had not had the capacity to feel pain.

The Capacity for Pleasure

- What kind of pleasurable animal experiences are we talking about? Ecstasy, contentment, or absence of pain? The utilitarian concept of happiness is applied to animal capacity for pleasure.

Who Should Be Saved?

- A practical criterion for a hierarchy of importance: the capacity for pain and pleasure, highest in humans.

Rationality as a Moral Criterion

What Is Rationality?

- A discussion of the concept of rationality, evident to eighteenth-century thinkers, but not any longer.

Who Is Rational?

- Kant's definition seems to exclude some humans and all animals.
- Animal rationality reconsidered in the light of new research, from Clever Hans the horse to Kanzi the bonobo chimpanzee.

SUGGESTION

Your students will probably also enjoy a discussion of whether animals can think rationally; pet owners should have some stories to tell. It is a good idea to advise the students to look at their own stories critically: Are they really examples of rational thinking, or are they examples of trained, mechanical responses? Here you may want to take up the discussion from Chapter 6 of whether the concept of rationality should be redefined.

- Kant's criterion opens up for the inclusion of nonhuman rational beings (hypothetical extraterrestrials, thinking computers, etc.).

Trees and Other Elements of Nature

- Hans Christian Andersen's fairy tale of Little Ida's Flowers asks what would happen if plants could communicate. Would we have to consider the rights of plants?
- Christopher Stone's views on the moral standing of the environment.

- A slippery slope argument: Can we allow ourselves to eat vegetables? Three ways to respond to a slippery slope: (1) leave our original position, (2) accept the consequences of the slope, or (3) dig into the slope by showing there is a relevant difference between the "steps" on the slope.

SUGGESTION

Your students may appreciate learning how to deal with a slippery slope argument. You may want to use the following example: The slope claims that if you refuse to kill animals for fur, then you must also stop eating animals, hunting animals for sport, or killing pests. The purpose of the slope argument may be twofold: It is probably a *reductio ad absurdum* designed to make you stop feeling guilty about wearing fur or eating meat, but it might also be a serious argument to convince you to hold all life sacred. Although you may agree that it is wrong to kill animals for fur or food, you might find arguments to support your view that it is not wrong to kill roaches and ants in your kitchen.

Some Solutions

- Justin Leiber's fictional example of the prospective termination of the intelligent computer and the chimpanzee for financial reasons.
- Mary Midgley's suggestion that the important criteria ought to be (1) the capacity for suffering and (2) the capacity for bonding.
- Bioethics as a relevant topic of the future.
- Reference to Chapter 20 and story outlines concerning the question of personhood: *Orphan of Creation*, *Blade Runner*, "The Circular Ruins," *Pinocchio*, and *Star Trek: The Next Generation:* "The Measure of a Man."

Boxes

What Does It Mean to Be Human? A list of popular definitions, such as "is two-legged," "has language," and so forth.

What Is a Fact? Discusses the nature of a "fact" and explains that so-called facts are the result of a selection of data that the person gathering data decides is relevant. What counts as a fact may depend on one's perspective.

The Beginnings of Slavery Slavery probably began with tribal prisoners of war.

Is a Fetus a Person? A brief introduction to the subject: the Catholic view of the person, from Saint Augustine to the homunculus theory, and the modern question of whether the personhood of the fetus is relevant in terms of the abortion debate.

You may want to have a class discussion about the subject of abortion at this point. Because the question is brought up in a chapter about personhood, it would be logical to base the debate on whether or not the right to abortion should depend on the personhood of the fetus and how much the personhood of the pregnant woman should count. You may want to add the following information to the class discussion of the homunculus theory: The observation was initially made by the young scholar De la Plantade (Dalenpatius) in 1693 and supposedly a year later by Hartsoeker. A scholar who is often assumed to have seen these homunculi, Leeuwenhoek, actually argued against the possibility of homunculi. For many this was part of a "male determination" theory, assuming that the male supplies the embryo, while the female egg only supplies nutrition for the growing embryo.

The Donner Party—Survival Statistics   Some facts about the ill-fated Donner Party of 1847: three-quarters of the female members survived.

Do Humans Always Count for More?   Arguments for speciesism (human chauvinism, homocentrism).

Chapter 15: Can We Decide Our Own Actions?

This chapter's theme is determinism versus free will, and it falls in two major sections: (1) the theories of determinism and behaviorism contrasted with compatibilism and Sartre's concept of free will, and (2) the principle of sociobiology represented by Darwin, Lorenz, and Ardrey. The second section contains a discussion of the naturalistic fallacy and concludes with a discussion of the cultural origin of humans: was the prime human invention the weapon or the basket?

I. Determinism Versus Free Will

Fatalism, Predestinarianism, and Karma

- Definition of fatalism as a religious theory assuming that everything happens according to fate.
- Somerset Maugham's story of the meeting in Samarra. The servant is fated to meet Death, even if he tries to avoid her.
- Definition of predestinarianism: Because of the original sin, all humans deserve eternal damnation; God, however, has already selected who will be saved.
- Definition of karma as a theological concept within the Hindu and Buddhist beliefs in reincarnation: a mechanistic consequence of past deeds or omissions.

Mechanistic Determinism

Prediction and Behavior Control

- Determinism is a mechanistic, nontheological idea that if we know enough about the causes of an event, we can predict its consequences. Theoretically, 100 percent knowledge would give 100 percent accuracy in predicting events.
- The principle of causality is the basis of determinism.
- Determinism precludes freedom of the will.
- B. F. Skinner's behaviorism is outlined: all human behavior is a matter of material influences—instinct, conditioning, or both. There is no mental realm.
- If there is no free will, then we cannot be held responsible for our actions.

Nature or Nurture?

- Nature means heredity, and nurture means environment. Research shows that both are important.
- Twins separated from birth often have similar lifestyles: This is an argument for "nature," not "nurture."

SUGGESTION

Students are likely to want to discuss the question of nature versus nurture at some length. Is upbringing more decisive than genetic makeup? Based on personal experiences, your students may have interesting contributions to make.

Determinism in Court: Leopold and Loeb—and Others

- The court case of Leopold and Loeb, who murdered a boy in order to commit the perfect crime. Their defense: Their actions were determined by their environment, and they could not be held responsible.

Everything Has a Cause

- The factors of heredity and environment are determining factors in our decision making.
- Is the freedom of the will something apart from heredity or environment? Usually we don't think a free decision is an uncaused one.

When Can We Be Held Responsible?

- Aristotle: Actions are involuntary if they are compulsory or a result of ignorance.
- Example of ignorance: Only when a situation cannot be foreseen can one claim ignorance as a valid excuse.

- Example of ignorance: Only when lack of knowledge about performing an action prevents one from performing that action can one claim ignorance.
- Examples of compulsion: A restricting, external force, a compulsory internal force, or unforeseen circumstances.

Answers to Determinism

Compatibilism

- W. T. Stace's explanation of compatibilism as a theory that allows determinism and free will to be compatible.

Self-Determination

- The causality of the mind allows for self-determination.

Freedom as Lived Experience

- We may be governed by heredity and environment, but because we are not aware of it and are aware that some of our decisions seem free, then that is what counts.

Indeterminism

- The theory of Jean-Paul Sartre is that humans can always choose another path than the one they are on, since the mental realm is not governed by causality.

SUGGESTION

In an interview, Sartre claimed that he was a determinist, but he still believed in total human freedom. You may want to ask your students how Sartre could reconcile these two statements.

- Problems with indeterminism: If all or part of the mental realm is outside of causality, we cannot rely on any decisions to take effect.

I Am Not You: Bergson's Solution

SUGGESTION

Bergson's theory of time and space is notoriously difficult for undergraduate students to get a grip on, especially on the basis of a brief presentation such as this. I have included this viewpoint because I find it an essential contribution to the debate, but my students generally have difficulties with it. I suggest that you go back to Chapter 11, to the box "Henri Bergson: Let Your True Self Emerge,"
(continued)

---

and combine the discussion of free will with Bergson's notion of the true self emerging, if your students are receptive. Otherwise, it may be wise to bypass the Bergson discussion altogether.

- Henri Bergson's reaction to determinism and indeterminism: Both are wrong, because both envision that the future is somehow mapped out already. The future is not a map existing in space with paths that can be chosen, but a potential in the mind of humans as temporal creatures.
- It is not possible for anyone to predict what others are going to do, because if they had that much knowledge about that person, they would be identical to that person.

Sartre: There Is No Human Nature

The Issue of Free Will

- A discussion of Sartre's view that humans are above having a nature; if humans assume they have a nature, they are reducing themselves to the status of beings who have no free will.
- Humans have existence for themselves (*pour soi*), whereas animals and things exist in themselves (*en soi*).
- Existence precedes essence: Humans determine their own essence, unlike for animals and things, where essence precedes existence.

Bad Faith, Anguish, and Choice

- Reintroducing bad faith: The illusion that we can decide not to choose.
- A choice for oneself is a choice for all humanity, even if we have to choose without being certain of the rightness of the outcome. Example: The student who has to decide whether to stay with his mother or join the resistance.

How Free Are We?

- Can we always decide to do something else? For Sartre this does not mean we can decide to be in a different situation, but we can decide how to relate to the situation we are in, such as refuse to follow orders.

SUGGESTION

There is no narrative section covering the subject of free will, because existentialism was covered in Chapter 13. However, you may want to point your students' attention to stories such as *A Few Good Men* (film, 1992) and *Like Water for Chocolate* (novel and film, 1991) as illustrations of the phenomenon of following orders.

- As we can change our perception of the situation we are in, we can change our interpretation of the past, according to the changing present.
- Reference to Chapter 20 and story outlines concerning the question of determinism and free will: "The Ugly Duckling," "Flight of the Eagle," and *The Wild Child.*

II. *Sociobiology: Determinism Applied*

The Principle of Sociobiology

- Sociobiology is defined as a theory of human social life based on biological theory.

Darwin's Legacy

Natural Selection

- The theory of the survival of the fittest and the consequences for a philosophy of human nature: gene promotion.

Criticism of Darwin's Ideas

- How exactly to interpret "survival of the fittest"? And are humans really all that well adapted?
- If humanity is evolving, is it becoming more ruthless or more gentle?
- Discussion of the argument that Darwin uses economic metaphors for his biological theory.
- Introduction of the concept of sociobiology.

Cain's Children: Konrad Lorenz and Robert Ardrey

- Lorenz and Ardrey arguing for the viewpoint that human beings are by nature aggressive.
- Ardrey: The invention of the weapon is what has made humans develop a higher intelligence.
- Criticism of Ardrey's argument that humans must have war in order not to go into a decline: It is a straw man argument.

The Naturalistic Fallacy

- A reintroduction of the naturalistic fallacy: Ardrey and other sociobiologists are moving from a biological fact (an "is") to a political and moral rule (an "ought").
- The point is made that the naturalistic fallacy can be used in a discriminatory way, even if the intentions are good.
- One can use facts to establish a rule or a policy, but not directly: One has to insert a value statement that is not derived from the fact.

The Weapon or the Basket? Leakey and Goodall

- Richard Leakey provides a countertheory to the idea that the weapon is the great cultural enhancer. For Leakey it is the invention of the basket that is the beginning of culture.

SUGGESTION

Students will generally be divided (and not always along gender lines!) as to whether they believe the weapon or the basket is the primary cultural invention. You might try to take a poll and discuss the results, or have the class divide into two groups and discuss the issue among themselves. An extremely lively format is to have the class physically divide into two groups and call out arguments to each other. Whenever someone changes his or her mind, have them walk over to the other group. This way the students learn not only about the force of arguments but also about rhetoric and peer pressure, especially if one group is significantly smaller to begin with and significantly larger at the end. This format works for all antagonistic issues, of course, but there is rarely time for this kind of discussion format more than once per semester.

- Jane Goodall's studies of chimpanzees conclude that chimpanzees are aggressive, but also caring. The conclusion for human nature is that we share those tendencies, but because humans are more than their biological tendencies, it doesn't lead to determinism.
- Reference to Chapter 20 and a story outline concerning the question of determinism and human aggression: *2001, A Space Odyssey.*

Boxes

What Is Free Will?   Definition of the philosophical problem of free will. Do we have free will at all—never, some of the time, or all the time?

The Indeterminism of Quantum Physics   Quantum physics does not operate with a principle of full determinability, since particles at the subatomic level are not predictable in all aspects.

SUGGESTION

Some of your students may be interested in *chaos theory*, the scientific theory that the future is essentially unpredictable because of the chaotic structure of underlying reality. You may want to point out that this theory is not in itself a refutation of determinism, but essentially based on the premises of determinism: Chaos theory does not claim that nothing can be predicted, only that some systems are so complex that it is impossible to foresee future events, such as the weather which can never, even in principle, be predicted with 100 percent
(continued)

---

accuracy because there are too many unforeseeable factors at play. However, it is precisely because of the existence of causality that these factors cannot be predicted, not because of any absence of causality. The weather pattern may be disturbed by a minor turbulence caused by something seemingly insignificant—a flutter of a butterfly's wings or a sneeze—but which will have great effects on future events.

The Lion as Metaphor   Discussion of whether Ardrey's image of the lion can be used as a metaphor for early humans.

SUGGESTION

It is my experience that many students have no conception of what a metaphor is. Here you may want to use an example, such as "My boyfriend is a tiger"/"My girlfriend is a fox." The metaphor expresses an identity, but not a literal one: You describe something by using the image of something else. (You may want to explain that if you had said, "My boyfriend is *like* a tiger," it would not have been a metaphor, but a simile.)

Chapter 16: Different Gender, Different Nature, Different Ethics?

This chapter raises the question of whether there are major morally relevant differences between women and men. The question of gender equality is discussed, in particular in light of the preceding discussion on sociobiology. A section on past views on women gives an overview of philosophical viewpoints on the gender issue, and the contemporary debates on feminism are shown to branch off in two major directions: one that views men and women as persons first and foremost (represented by Beauvoir), and one that sees men and women as fundamentally different, but equal (represented by Gilligan).

Main Points

What Is Gender Equality?

Gender and Language

- The shift from gender-specific to gender-neutral language is outlined and discussed.

SUGGESTION

As you may be aware, Dr. Virginia Warren of California State University, Long Beach, has authored a guide to avoidance of gender-specific terms in the field of philosophy, published by the APA. I have used these guidelines myself as an instructional device when discussing term papers and essay tests with my students, and for many students it is an eye-opening process. The idea that
(continued)

---

language can affect one's thinking (that gender-specific terms may subconsciously affect one's outlook on gender equality) is novel to many students, and a class discussion on the subject is usually a lively experience.

Is Biology Destiny?

- Two questions are implied: (1) Is there cultural/social equality? (normative) and (2) Is there biological equality? (descriptive).
- The implications of a sociobiological approach.

Past Views on Women

Women's Role in the Public Sector

- Women's traditional role in the private sphere and lack of influence in the public sphere.
- The duality of men protecting women and regarding them as property.

Some Philosophers on the Status of Women

- The views of Plato, Aristotle, Saint Augustine, Kant (with quote), Rousseau (with quote), Nietzsche (with quotes), Wollstonecraft (with quote), J. S. Mill (with quote), and Engels (with brief quote).

Contemporary Views on Gender Equality

The Two Facets of Gender Equality

- A brief history of Western feminism in the twentieth century.
- A shift in feminism from a focus on access to jobs and equal pay to a focus on women's special qualities.

Men and Women Are Persons

- Classical feminism is represented by Simone de Beauvoir: Woman is seen by man, and by herself, as "the Other," an atypical person, and the only way women can become authentic persons is to leave their role as deviant human beings through receiving the same education and treatment as men receive. When that happens, most of the gender differences will disappear.
- The consequence: androgynism as a political ideal. Joyce Trebilcot: mono-androgynism (everyone in a society ought to share all the best characteristics of both genders) rejected in favor of polyandrogynism (everyone in a society is free to choose his or her gender role).
- An ultimate version of androgynism: changing human biology through surgery.

- Research with children is inconclusive: When children are treated in a gender-neutral way, some opt for playing gender-neutral games or games typical of the opposite sex, but most seem to choose the traditional games of their own sex.

Men and Women Are Fundamentally Different

- The new feminism focuses on the fundamental differences between men and women and seeks a reevaluation in favor of women's qualities.
- Key argument: Science has treated man as the typical human being and woman as deviant or nonexisting. Both genders ought to be equally representative of the human race, including their differences.
- Carol Gilligan as representative of the new feminism: Men and women have different moral attitudes, and one is as correct as the other. Men tend toward an ethics of justice and rights, whereas women tend toward an ethics of caring.
- The Heinz dilemma as illustration of Gilligan's point.

Consequences of the Gender Debate

- The result of Gilligan's theory: Many women find themselves in agreement. Support from Deborah Tannen's research.
- A critical analysis of the consequences of Gilligan's theory: It may polarize the gender issue and make it harder for women to achieve equality in the workplace, and it may result in discrimination against male qualities.
- Reference to Chapter 20 and story outlines concerning the question of gender relations: "Men and Women Try Living Apart" and "The River of Separation," *The Temple of My Familiar*, *Foucault's Pendulum*, and *Thelma and Louise*.

Boxes

The Issue Is Manhole Covers   Examples of gender-specific and gender-neutral terms are used in a discussion of how much we should change our terminology.

Sex or Gender?   An explanation of the shift in terminology from "sex" to "gender."

French Salons: An Important Influence   The important role of women hostesses in the development of French philosophy and politics before the French Revolution.

Early Feminism in France   The prerevolution debate introduced by Poulain de la Barre, a student of Descartes.

The Other: Simone de Beauvoir   A biography of Beauvoir, an evaluation of her philosophical connection with Sartre, and an evaluation of her role in the recent feminist debate.

Can Gays Choose Not To Be Gay?   A discussion of whether homosexuality is a matter of biology or a choice of lifestyle. Tentative scientific results point toward it being a biological phenomenon. Consequences for the debate are outlined.

Chapter 17: Are We Good or Evil from the Beginning?

This chapter presents four major Western philosophical viewpoints on whether humans are fundamentally good or evil: (1) the Christian viewpoint, represented by Saint Augustine, (2) the materialistic viewpoint of Hobbes, including his view of the State, (3) the romantic viewpoint of Rousseau, including his views of history and politics, and (4) the iconoclastic viewpoint of Nietzsche, including his views of the master and the slave and his theory of the eternal return.

Main Points

Introduction

- Biology can only tell us that we have tendencies toward compassion and aggression, but we are still looking for the ultimate answer to the question whether humans are fundamentally good or evil.

The Christian Viewpoint

The Original Sin

- The classical Christian doctrine of the original sin.
- The ambiguity in Saint Augustine: Is sexual human nature evil? An introduction to the philosophy of Augustine.

Redemption

- The original sin of Adam redeemed through Jesus Christ.

The Fall as Metaphor

- The Fall from the Garden of Eden is seen as an ethical metaphor that humans are by nature weak and evil.
- Association between innocent childhood and the Garden of Eden, and beginning sexual activity and the Fall.

Consequences and Criticism

- Political and theological consequences: Humans cannot be trusted to govern themselves.
- Elaine Pagel's criticism of Augustine, with quote. Pagels: Humans choose to believe they are guilty, because that means they have power to cause a great calamity by losing access to Paradise. Example of anthropocentrism.
- Reference to Chapter 20 and story outlines concerning the question of the dual human nature of good and evil: *Strange Case of Dr. Jekyll and Mr. Hyde,* "The Shadow," and *Crime and Punishment.*

Hobbes: Self-Interested Humanity

A Short Digression into the Concept of Metaphysics

- Reintroducing the concept of metaphysics, a detailed presentation of monism (idealism and materialism) and dualism.
- Introduction of the concept of identity theory and epiphenomenalism.
- A brief discussion of the dualistic theories of parallelism and interactionism, with mention of the problem of "the ghost in the machine."

Hobbes the Materialist

- Thomas Hobbes's materialistic theory of psychology: psychological egoism and determinism.

The State of Nature and the Social Contract

- Hobbes's theory of the state of nature: A presocial state of affairs where humans live in constant fear of each other (with quote).
- The social contract theory: A mutual agreement to end the fear of the state of nature by abiding by rules.
- Was the state of nature ever a historical reality?

SUGGESTION

Here you may want to discuss the Constitution of the United States as an example of a social contract. It is also possible to bring in John Locke's political philosophy here and speculate on whether people, as citizens, sign an implicit "social contract" merely by living in a society and taking advantage of its opportunities, and whether it is still possible to "opt out," as Locke suggested, and go live elsewhere if one disagrees with the rules.

- A comparison between Hobbes's theory of the social contract and Plato's *Republic* (see Chapter 8) where Glaucon expresses an identical view for the sake of argument.
- The role of the sovereign: The sovereign must ensure that the social contract is kept and may then rule single-handedly over the subjects.

The State of Nature as Political Theory

- It is a question whether Hobbes viewed the state of nature as evil or value-neutral.
- The political consequences: an argument in favor of monarchy.
- An evaluation of the historical correctness of Hobbes's theory: Humans have never lived in a solitary state such as Hobbes's vision of a presocial situation.

- Reference to Chapter 20 and a story outline concerning the question of whether human nature is at bottom selfish and evil: *Lord of the Flies*.

SUGGESTION

You may want to mention to your class that politicians and others with political influence often assume that humans are by nature evil. Eleanor Roosevelt, the wife of President F. D. Roosevelt, once expressed the opinion that in order to live up to the Declaration of Human Rights, human nature had to be changed. You might ask your students to outline what kind of political systems may arise from such a viewpoint.

Rousseau: Back to Nature

Arrival of the Enlightenment

- A brief outline of the historical changes from the time of Hobbes to the time of Jean-Jacques Rousseau.

Rousseau, the Traveling Man

- A biography of Rousseau.

Before Rousseau: "Natural" Equals "Evil"

- The attitude toward nature from Augustine to the time of Rousseau: Nature is evil, or godless, and must be controlled.
- Four aspects of this attitude: (1) a practical level: nature is dangerous; (2) a theological level: humans are rulers of creation, and nature must be subdued; (3) an economic level: nature is meaningful only if it can be used for a profit; (4) a psychological level: as nature is an evil that must be controlled, so must human desires be controlled.

Rousseau: "Natural" Equals "Good"

- With Rousseau, nature is viewed as good in itself.
- The Romantic Movement and the term *back to nature*.
- Four aspects of this attitude: (1) a psychological level: emotions are more genuine and natural than reason; (2) an ethical level: animals and children come to represent moral innocence; (3) a historical level: the "noble savage" is admired; (4) a political level: civilization is viewed as a corrupting force.

Humans in the State of Nature

- Rousseau's version of the state of nature: Humans are happy, healthy, and solitary. Quote from the second *Discourse*.

- In nature, humans are naturally compassionate. There is physical, but no social, inequality; that begins with the conception of property. Quote from the second *Discourse*.

The Social Contract and Beyond

- In Rousseau's social contract theory, people don't give away their sovereignty, contrary to Hobbes's theory.

- The general will ensures that all decisions have the general welfare in mind.

- Criticism of Rousseau's concept of the general will: No possibility of civil disobedience in a true democracy, since it can never be right to go against the general will. Hard to determine what constitutes majority opinion.

History and Politics

- Evaluation of the historical correctness of Rousseau's theory: Humans were never solitary, but pretechnological tribal populations live under conditions closer to those described by Rousseau than to those described by Hobbes.

Should We Stop Thinking?

- Does Rousseau advocate going back to nature? No, but he suggests learning from nature and raising children in a more natural way.

- Reference to Chapter 20 and a story outline concerning the idea that nature is good in itself: *Dances with Wolves*.

Nietzsche: Beyond Good and Evil

The Masters of Suspicion

- Paul Ricoeur's theory of the three masters of suspicion: Nietzsche, Marx, and Freud.

Nietzsche's Background

- A biography of Nietzsche.

Nietzsche's Suspicion: Beyond Good and Evil

- Nietzsche's critique of the Western tradition of Christian and Platonic legacy. His transvaluation of values, changing from the historically repressive values of Christianity to life-affirming values of power.
- All values are a matter of perspectivism: There is no absolute moral truth except the value that affirms life.

The Master and the Slave

- Nietzsche's vision of the early morals of a feudal society: the master morality versus the slave morality. Quote from *The Genealogy of Morals*.
- The nobleman as a creator of power and values; the slave morality as a morality of resentment toward the powerful and capable master.
- With Christianity the slave morality took over and banished the master morality; in addition, the slave morality has been carried on by utilitarianism and socialism.

The Overman

- The slave morality denies life, but a transvaluation of slave values will allow new "masters" to set their own higher standards: the Overmen (Supermen).
- An evaluation of Nietzsche's concept of the transvaluation of values: a positive aspect—attacking the double standards of the nineteenth century and its denial of physical pleasures; a negative aspect—Nietzsche's influence on the Nazi ideology and its concept of a master race.
- Would Nietzsche have approved of Hitler? Probably not, because he would have seen Hitler as a "slave," full of resentment.

The Eternal Return and the Value of Life

- The famous saying that "God is dead."
- Discussion whether or not Nietzsche was a nihilist.
- Two theories of the doctrine of the eternal return: (1) Nietzsche believed that everything returns exactly the same way, and thus everything is meaningless. (2) Nietzsche used the idea of the return as a test for how much one loves life, even if it should repeat itself endlessly.

SUGGESTION

You might ask your students if they could pass this test of saying yes to life: Would they want their lives to be endlessly repeated?

- Reference to Chapter 20 and story outlines concerning the idea of the eternal return of the same: *The Myth of Sisyphus, Thus Spoke Zarathustra*, and *Replay*.

Boxes

Manichaeism and Neoplatonism   A brief outline of Manichaeism (good and evil locked in battle) and Neoplatonism (the emanation of spiritual force from God to human souls).

Loss of Immortality: Placing Blame   A selection of stories from world mythology in which the responsibility for introducing mortality to humans is placed on a woman.

The Life and Times of Thomas Hobbes   The violent history of Hobbes's day and age, and his own attempt to stay safe.

The Eighteenth Century: A Time of Persecution   An explanation of the reasons behind Rousseau's fears of persecution. The power of the Inquisition, and the rise of secret scientific and political societies.

Nature in Art   An overview of the changing appreciation of nature in Western art from the Middle Ages to Rousseau.

Ricoeur: To Suspect and to Listen   Ricoeur's hermeneutic principle of criticism: a suspecting attitude combined with a listening approach.

Elisabeth Nietzsche and the Nazis   Nietzsche's sister Elisabeth's role in Nietzsche's life, and her influence on the Nazi party in the 1930s.

Perspectivism and Postmodernism   Nietzsche's theory of perspectivism and its influence on the philosophical and cultural movement of postmodernism.

Hegel and the Master-Slave Dialectic   Hegel's analysis of the interdependence between the master and the slave from *The Phenomenology of the Spirit*.

Chapter 18: The Soul and the State

Four thinkers are represented here, each representing an influential view of the human psyche and its relation to its political environment: Plato's theory of the tripartite soul and the ideal state, Aristotle's theory of man as a "political animal," Marx's view of human nature under capitalism and under communism, and Freud's theory of the Unconscious and in particular the Oedipus complex.

Main Points

Plato, the Soul, and the State

The Nature of Reality: Changing or Unchanging?

- A reintroduction of Plato's theory of Forms as a dualistic, metaphysical theory.
- Two schools of metaphysics: True reality is unchanging versus true reality is changing.

The Soul

- Plato's theory of the tripartite soul: reason, spirit, and desires.
- The image of the charioteer from Phaedrus.
- Plato's theory of reincarnation.

The State

- The tripartite structure of the ideal state: the Guardians, the Auxiliaries, and the working population. Society as an organism, with philosopher kings as leaders.

Aristotle: Man Is a Political Animal

Teleology and Theory of Causation

- Reintroduction of Aristotle's theory of teleology and causation (four causes: material, efficient, formal, final).

Man, the Political Animal

- Excerpt from Aristotle's *Politics*: The state is a natural creation, and man is a social being.
- Discussion of Aristotle's political theory: The state is a social given.
- Excerpt from *Politics:* the ruler and the ruled; soul and body; humans and animals; males and females.
- Discussion of excerpt, with emphasis on Aristotle's theory of slavery.

Karl Marx: Human Nature Will Change

Marx as a Materialist

- Marx's philosophy of dialectical materialism. A brief biography of Marx, with emphasis on the legacy of Hegel and the theory of dialectics.
- Hegel: History is the development of the spirit. Marx: History consists of movements within economic development—a material development.
- Marx as a master of suspicion: The superstructure is determined by the underlying economic system.

Why Communism?

- Marx and Engels's collaboration, and Marx's reaction to nineteenth-century European working-class conditions.
- The theory of surplus value, and the realization of labor.
- The result of the realization of labor is alienation of the worker. Immediate causes: private property and division of labor.

Human Nature and Capitalism

- The ideal work situation: self-activity through meaningful work. Capitalism has robbed the working class of its self-activity (work-pleasure).

Human Nature and the Socialist System

- The economic basis of society must be changed to regain fairness and work-pleasure.
- The revolution must be universal and must come from the working class, not farmers.
- The slogan "To each according to need, from each according to ability" is analyzed.
- With a communistic economy, human nature will change.

SUGGESTION ————————————

You might ask your students if they are convinced: Will human nature change under a different economic system? Will all of human nature change? And why would it change?

Objections to Marx's Theory

- Discussion of nine major objections to Marxist theory: (1) Communism has been tried, and it didn't work. (2) If the revolution happens automatically, why work for it? (3) If the human mind is determined by society, how can it be critical of society? (4) If history moves in a dialectical pattern, why should communism be the final one? (5) How can everybody have meaningful work in the communist society? (6) What is the incentive to work harder if you get what you need? (7) Isn't self-preservation a biological fact? (8) Will all of human nature change with the advent of communism, including reason? (9) Perhaps Marx's vision was reasonable in the nineteenth century, but we don't need it anymore.
- Herbert Marcuse's neo-Marxist theory of repressive tolerance and indoctrination.
- Reference to Chapter 20 and story outlines illustrating political viewpoints: "Harrison Bergeron," *The Grapes of Wrath*, and *Atlas Shrugged*.

Sigmund Freud: We Don't Know Ourselves

The Birth of Psychoanalysis

- The three blows to the human self-assurance: Copernicus, Darwin, and Freud.
- Research in psychology before Freud.
- Freud's biography and his work in hysteria theory.

Dreams Are Wishes

- Freud's *Interpretation of Dreams*, and his theory that dreams are wish fulfillment.
- The theory of repression of traumatic experiences.

Other Manifestations of the Unconscious

- The Freudian slip (parapraxis), with examples. Parapraxes reveal hidden motivations.

SUGGESTION

Since everybody has stories of experiences with Freudian slips, your students may enjoy sharing theirs, either in a relaxed discussion format or in a term paper. If you choose to incorporate a question about personal experiences with Freudian slips, you might encourage the students to search for a possible latent meaning in the manifest occurrence; however, they should be aware that (1) there may not be such a meaning, because Freud may not be right in his theory; (2) if there is a latent meaning, it is not certain that we can find it ourselves without the aid of an analyst, and it may do more harm than good to play at interpreting our own slips as well as those of others. (I'd like to share a Freudian slip of my own with you: Several times while writing the Freud section of *The Moral of the Story*, I found myself typing the word *Fraud*, instead of *Freud*. . . . I have much respect for Freud, and I tend to believe that the typo reflects my lack of skill as a typist rather than anything deeper; however, it just may reveal certain personal reservations!)

- For Freud a mistake is no accident if a meaning can be found, so whenever we can point to a hidden meaning in a mistake, then that mistake is a parapraxis.

The Oedipus Complex

- A brief account of the tragedy of King Oedipus, and the story in relation to the Oedipus complex: the boy's bonding with his mother and fear of his father.
- The little girl and the so-called Electra complex.
- The pleasure principle and the reality principle.

Id, Ego, and Superego

- Freud's tripartite theory of the psyche: Id (the Unconscious), Ego (the sense of self), and the Super-ego (the conscience).
- The three masters of the Ego: the reality principle, the Id, and the Superego.
- A comparison between Freud's and Plato's theories of the soul.

74

Social Consequences of Freud's Theory of Human Nature

- Social consequences of Freud's theory of the Unconscious are social repression and sublimation of drives.
- Different reactions from later psychoanalysts: Jung (the collective unconscious is a creative source, not a threat) and Reich (Marx and Freud combined in a sexual and political revolutionary theory).

Humans and Religion

- Freud's theory of the primal horde, an early group of young men killing the old man monopolizing the women.
- The killing of the old man being the cause of religion: guilt leads to worshipping.

Objections to Freud's Theories

- Criticism: The theory doesn't explain polytheism, and it doesn't explain the religious faith of women.
- Freud's theory of psychology reflects nineteenth-century family patterns: strong father-breadwinner, weak mother-homemaker. With other family structures, other complexes may develop.

SUGGESTION

Especially in terms of repression and family relationships, you may want to take up the subject of people in their adulthood suddenly remembering being abused as children, sometimes in connection with devil-worshipping rituals. It is commonly referred to as the syndrome of ritual child abuse. While some cases certainly reveal repressed, traumatic experiences from childhood, psychoanalysts and therapists are now beginning to realize that some of these "remembered" situations may not be true memories, but fantasies inadvertently implanted in the mind during hypnosis by well-meaning therapists, and parents and other caregivers find themselves the victims of witch hunts on the basis of such implanted memories. Whereas Freud seems to have believed that everything is stored in our memory like in a perfect recording, psychology today has abandoned this theory of memory as the perfect recorder; many memories are simply not recorded, and it may not be due to repression at all. Besides, scholars point out, a memory is not the experience itself, but a representation or an interpretation of an experience.

- Freud is a determinist, so does he think we can be held responsible for our acts?
- The concepts of denial and resistance make Freud's theory of psychoanalysis irrefutable.
- Reference to Chapter 20 and story outlines concerning the Unconscious: *Oedipus Rex* and *Marnie*.

Boxes

Metaphysics and Human Nature   Any view of human nature is based on an underlying theory of metaphysics. Theories of reality as unchanging versus theories of reality as changing.

Socrates on Self-Control in All Things, Including Love   The follow-up to the story of the charioteer in *Phaedrus:* self-control in passionate relationships.

A Mind Divided: Other Views of the Soul   Egyptian and shamanistic traditions are mentioned as examples of philosophies involving the concept of division of the soul into separate parts.

The Virtuous Person Recalled   Aristotle's theory of purpose seen in connection with a theory of human nature. The role of happiness in Aristotle's virtue theory, and Aristotle's concept of individual and political freedom.

Natural Law and Natural Inclinations   The theory of natural law is discussed with reference to the issue of whether Supreme Court Justice Clarence Thomas is a natural law theorist. A brief outline of natural law theory: a normative theory about human morality based on a theory of human God-given inclinations.

SUGGESTION

Because the concept of natural law is much broader than may appear in this box, you may want to discuss the subject further with your students and explain to them that natural law, aside from specifically signifying the theory of natural inclinations mentioned in the box, is a common term for the broader viewpoint that law and legal matters are fundamentally unrelated to human social conventions. Many natural law theorists believe law has a foundation in human nature, and human reason in particular. Some believe the foundation lies in a divinity. The theory is generally opposed to *legal positivism,* the view that law is a human invention, fundamentally based on social conventions and political power. For a legal positivist there is no such thing as a universal law that should be enforced, unless the world community can agree on it. A natural law theorist may well assume that certain universal laws should be enforced, regardless of social conventions. On the basis of this distinction between natural law and legal positivism your class may want to discuss the relevancy of asking a Supreme Court nominee whether he or she believes in natural law.

The Fail-Safe Nature of Hegel's Theory   Hegel believed that any stage of intellectual development has its own place in the development of the Spirit, so Hegel's critics have their own place, too.

Was Oedipus Real?   Robert Graves's theory that Oedipus may have been a sacrificial king married to a high priestess of Hera, who instigated a patriarchal, hereditary kingship tradition and was banished for it.

ELIZA: The Perfect Listener?   The computer program ELIZA imitates the questions a psychoanalyst would be likely to ask.

Chapter 19: The Storytelling Animal

This chapter takes up the theme from Part 1 with a discussion of current narrative theories. MacIntyre's concept of cultural narratives is presented and discussed, and the narrative theories of Ricoeur, White, and Nussbaum are examined and placed in the context of ethical theory. Lastly, the individual and cultural experience of telling stories as a way of structuring and evaluating one's life and experience is examined.

Main Points

MacIntyre's Call for Stories

- MacIntyre: The Western culture is morally confused because there is no common ethos of tradition.
- We must understand ourselves as part of a narrative whole: a storytelling tradition.
- Narrative selfhood is correlative: Our own story interacts with those of others.
- The quest for narrative selfhood is going back to virtue theory, and our culture determines the kind of virtues we should look for.
- Criticism of MacIntyre: The list of virtues is limited, the idea of a dominant culture is uncomfortable, rationality is neglected, and ethical relativism is a consequence.

Narrative Theory: Ricoeur, White, and Nussbaum

Paul Ricoeur: Time and Narrative

- Aristotle's theory about the function of cleansing literature: A good story follows the structure of a plot.
- Paul Ricoeur's theory of narrativity and time identifies three levels to a story: (1) the simple plot structure, (2) the chronological reading of the plot as entertainment, and (3) the understanding of the story, grasped as a whole. In the third level we experience the story as a personal involvement.
- Narrative time: the time frame of the story that we experience during reading.

Hayden White: History Is Storytelling

- White: History-writing is related to storytelling.
- Example: The "discovery" of America by Columbus is a story told from a viewpoint, with a subjective selection of evidence.
- Nietzsche's concept of perspectivism applied to White's view of historiography.
- The postmodern view of history is one of perspectivism: There is not one absolute viewpoint, but a multitude of equally valid perspectives.
- Not all history-writing has been done in story form. For example: annals.

- For the modern Western mind, history must work like a story in order to seem as if it is making sense: We choose a beginning that will determine the middle and the end, and we look for the "why," the cause of an event.
- For White all stories including history-writing make a moral statement.
- A discussion of whether White is Eurocentric in his philosophy.

SUGGESTION

If the debate about multiculturalism is interesting to you and your students, you may consider talking about the subjects of perspectivism and Eurocentrism here, and remind the students of Chapter 3 (the debate about relativism and multiculturalism). A personal comment: Being a European, I find the concept of Eurocentrism particularly interesting—and a misnomer. The American mainstream culture is not Eurocentric in the sense that it is concerned with, or knowledgeable about, European history or conditions except in the sense that European history relates to American history. This is, if anything, an "Americentric" attitude. And, since American demographics are changing, it is natural to expect this attitude to expand and encompass the relevant histories of the immigrant non-European population (and if it doesn't expand, it probably should!).

Martha Nussbaum: Living Other Lives

- Nussbaum is interested in the emotional force of narratives.
- Emotions have cognitive value and are, as a rule, not irrational, nor do they happen at random.
- Why have philosophers refused to deal seriously with emotions? Because when humans experience emotions they are immersed in life that affects them and cannot be considered rationally autonomous.
- Emotions are our best access to values, and their clearest manifestation is in narratives.
- There are different narratives in different cultures, but this need not lead to cultural relativism.
- Why stories, and not designed philosophical examples instead? Because the rich texture of the story is what we relate to, and narratives are more open-ended than philosophical examples.
- Quote: We need stories in order to live other lives vicariously, because we have never lived enough to understand life and each other.
- Also, it is sometimes easier to discuss stories with others than talk about private moments in our own lives.

78

- We don't want the unchanging world of autonomous reason, but the real, changing world that we are emotionally engaged in.

The Story as Life Experience

Living in Time

- The temporal structure of the mind: remembering the past, anticipating the future.
- With the temporal experience comes the awareness of mortality.

When Bad Things Happen

- Erikson's concept of ego integrity; the challenge to ego integrity when something unexpected and bad happens.
- Ways of dealing with such an occurrence: (1) to see it as the hand of God, or fate; (2) to interpret it as karma from past lives; (3) to see it as the sufferer's own fault.

Life as a Story

- An alternate way (4): Stories help us to deal emotionally with the unexpected.
- The stories of traditional cultures may teach a different lesson than stories in modern cultures.
- The identity crisis arises when life doesn't make sense anymore, due to bad and unforeseen events.
- The help of narratives: We can rewrite our own story and find a new meaning by reinterpreting past events and see them in a new pattern, a new "plot."

Living in the Narrative Zone

- Humans are temporal, living their own story between beginning and end, as well as living the stories of their culture.
- The life-expanding experience of narrative time: We can retain our own life while sharing in the accelerated time of books and films.
- Stories, experienced in the right amount, can help us make decisions and avoid mistakes.
- Ursula LeGuin and the metaphor of the hoop snake that bites its own tail: Storytelling is important, if it is combined with action and taking a chance, even if you may get hurt in the process.
- Reference to the story outlines in *The Moral of the Story* as illustration of the importance of stories. A warning that outlines are not enough to experience the "narrative zone."

There is a category of stories not mentioned in *The Moral of the Story*, but one that I find intriguing as a meta-analysis of the project of using stories to illustrate philosophical issues: stories that in some way explore the moral importance of storytelling itself. If some of your students have enjoyed being exposed to stories with a philosophical point, you might suggest for them to do a research paper examining this phenomenon. A list of such stories may include the following titles:

Karen Blixen (Isak Dinesen), "The Blank Page," short story (1957); "The Cardinals' First Tale," short story (1957).

Ayn Rand, "The Simplest Thing in the World," shot story (1967).

The French Lieutenant's Woman, film (1981).

Kim Stanley Robinson, *The Wild Shore*, novel (1984).

Isabelle Allende, *Eva Luna*, novel (1987).

Box

Movies, Too? Nussbaum has as little interest in films as Ricoeur does, but her theory opens up for an inclusion of films as narrative experiences.

Chapter 20: Narratives of Human Nature

This final chapter provides the narrative discussion material for Chapters 14–18.

- The issue of personhood (Chapter 14) is illustrated by the novel *Orphan of Creation*, the film *Blade Runner*, the short story "The Circular Ruins," the cartoon feature *Pinocchio*, and an episode from *Star Trek: The Next Generation*: "The Measure of a Man."

- The question of "nature or nurture?" (Chapter 15) is posed in the following stories representing both determinism and sociobiology: the short stories "The Ugly Duckling" and "Flight of the Eagle," the film *The Wild Child*, and the film *2001, A Space Odyssey*.

- The issue of gender differences (Chapter 16) is explored by the myths of "Men and Women Try Living Apart" and "The River of Separation," the novels *The Temple of My Familiar* and *Foucault's Pendulum*, and the film *Thelma and Louise*.

- The question of whether humans are good or evil (Chapter 17) is presented in the stories the *Strange Case of Dr. Jekyll and Mr. Hyde* and "The Shadow" and the novels *Crime and Punishment* and *Lord of the Flies*. The film *Dances with Wolves* represents Rousseau's viewpoint that everything natural is good.

- The Nietzschean topic of the eternal return of the same (Chapter 17) is represented by the myth of Sisyphus, Nietzsche's visionary novel *Thus Spoke Zarathustra*, and the science fiction novel *Replay*.

- Finally, Sophocles's tragedy of *Oedipus Rex* and the film *Marnie* serve as illustrations of Freudian theory (Chapter 18), and the short story "Harrison Bergeron," the novel and film *The Grapes of Wrath*, and the novel *Atlas Shrugged* discuss the topic of politics (Chapter 18): Can the vision of socialism and communism give hope to the working population?

Personhood

- The following outlines explore the subject of the criterion for being a person and having human rights.
- Roger McBride Allen's novel *Orphan of Creation* (1988) tells of an African-American paleoanthropologist who discovers a surviving remnant of a prehominid population thought to be extinct for a million years, and society is faced with the decision whether to use these beings as slaves, put them in a zoo, perform experiments on them, or grant them human rights.
- In the film *Blade Runner* (1982), a private detective has the job of hunting down and destroying artificial humans (replicants) who are a threat to real humans, and the film speculates about what constitutes a real human.
- In "The Circular Ruins," a short story by Jorge Luis Borges (1941), a man is able to magically create another man by concentrated dreaming, but has second thoughts because he finds the idea of being created by another one's mind humiliating. However, soon he realizes that he himself is nothing but a dream of someone else's mind.
- In the cartoon feature film *Pinocchio* (1940), a good fairy gives life to the wooden puppet Pinocchio and promises him that he will become a real boy if he is good, but Pinocchio has no sense of good and evil. Eventually he redeems himself through an act of bravery and altruism.
- In *Star Trek: The Next Generation*: "The Measure of a Man," Data, the android Starfleet officer, is told he must submit to a research procedure that may rob him of his personality, and he refuses. A trial ensues in order to determine whether Data is a machine, the property of Starfleet, or a person with the right to self-determination.

SOME ADDITIONAL NARRATIVES ILLUSTRATING
THE QUESTION OF PERSONHOOD

Henrik Ibsen, *Peer Gynt*, play (1867).

Luigi Pirandello, *Six Characters in Search of an Author*, play (1921).

Wizard of Oz, film (1939).

Cordwainer Smith, "The Ballad of Lost C'Mell," short story (1962); "The Dead Lady of Clown Town," short story (1964).

2001, A Space Odyssey, film (1968). Concerns the character of HAL, the computer.

Johnny Got His Gun, film (1971).

Cordwainer Smith, *Norstrilia*, novel (1975).

Barry B. Longyear, *Enemy Mine*, short story (1979). Better than the film.

Elephant Man, film (1980).

Children of a Lesser God, film (1986).

Rain Man, film (1988).

Rebecca Ore, *Becoming Alien*, *Being Alien*, and *Human to Human* (trilogy of novels 1988–90).

Nature or Nurture?

- Hans Christian Andersen's "The Ugly Duckling" (1844) versus Henrik Pontoppidan's "Flight of the Eagle" (1894). The famous Andersen story tells of a baby swan that happens to grow up among ducks in perpetual harassment because he is different; as he matures into a swan and finds his own kind, he realizes that it is one's true nature that is important. The Pontoppidan "counterstory," on the other hand, tells of a baby eagle growing up in a farmyard. The day comes when the eagle gets a chance to fulfill his eagle nature, but he has lost this nature due to his upbringing among the lowly ducks and chickens.

- The film *The Wild Child* (1969) tells the true story of a researcher who tries to educate a feral child in eighteenth-century France. Although the boy is capable of learning a few things, it seems that his human nature is lost because of lack of training in the formative years.

SUGGESTION

The study-question section to *The Wild Child* contains a brief introduction to the historical debate between empiricists and rationalists. If you think your students might profit from an extensive discussion of this topic, you may want to illustrate the subject further by comparing John Locke's empiricism (possibly in connection with Berkeley and Hume) with Descartes's rationalism, and include Kant's theory of knowledge as an alternative theory. You may want to discuss Noam Chomsky's theory of language acquisition as a modern version of a Kantian approach. I did not include these subjects in the text itself because I wanted to limit the discussion to questions of ethics and human nature.

- The film *2001, A Space Odyssey* (1968) has several features that are relevant to Part 4. The personhood of HAL the computer is one, but here we look at another: the theory that humans developed their intelligence in the process of using weapons.

SOME ADDITIONAL NARRATIVES ILLUSTRATING THE QUESTION OF DETERMINISM AND FREE WILL

John Steinbeck, *East of Eden*, novel (1950). Clearer discussion of free will in the novel than in the film.

Compulsion, film (1959) about Leopold and Loeb.

A Few Good Men, film (1992).

Swoon, film (1992). About Leopold and Loeb, but without the focus on determinism.

SOME ADDITIONAL NARRATIVES ILLUSTRATING
THE QUESTION OF HUMAN NATURE AND AGGRESSION

The Quiet Man, film (1952).

William Golding, *Lord of the Flies*, novel (1954). *Lord of the Flies* is also outlined below as an example of evil human nature.

Zardoz, film (1974).

Men and Women: Different Worlds?

- This section illustrates different perceptions of male and female human nature.
- "Men and Women Try Living Apart" and "The River of Separation," both Native American narratives but with different endings, tell of a mythical experiment in the early days of humanity: Women claimed they could live without men, so the men left them to live on the other side of the river. After some years the women admitted that they couldn't live without men.
- From Alice Walker's novel *The Temple of My Familiar* (1989) I have selected a story within the story: a pseudo-myth of the first men and the first women. The men envied the women of their power to give life, so they decided that they, the men, were the ones who should be considered the life-givers.
- The philosopher Umberto Eco's novel *Foucault's Pendulum* (1989) exposes the fascination for secret societies as a flight from life, and life is symbolized by the pregnant woman. Excerpt from *Foucault's Pendulum* claims that the secret of life is understood by women, not men: It is the process of life being created and lived.
- The film *Thelma and Louise* (1991) tells of two women who, due to a set of unforeseen circumstances, find themselves on the road to being criminals. During their car ride from Arkansas to New Mexico they face questions of their own identity and roles as women.

SOME ADDITIONAL NARRATIVES ILLUSTRATING
THE QUESTION OF MALE AND FEMALE HUMAN NATURE

Henrik Ibsen, *A Doll's House*, play (1879).

August Strindberg, *Getting Married*, play (1884).

Adam's Rib, film (1949).

Masculine Feminine, film (1966).

Seven Women, film (1966).

Alice Walker, *The Color Purple*, novel (1982) and film (1985).

Swing Shift, film (1984).

Margaret Atwood, *A Handmaid's Tale*, novel (1985). Better than the film.

Sheri S. Tepper, *Raising the Stones*, novel (1990).

He Said, She Said, film (1991).

SOME STORIES WITH A TWIST TO THE GENDER SUBJECT

Some Like It Hot, film (1939).

La Cage Aux Folles, film (1978).

Yentl, film (1983).

The Crying Game, film (1992).

Star Trek: The Next Generation: "The Outcast" (1992). An androgynous society discriminates against heterosexual behavior.

The Story of Little Jo, film (1993).

Are We Good or Evil?

- In this section, stories of a dual nature of a human individual illustrate the question of good versus evil human nature.

The Alter Ego

- Robert Louis Stevenson's novel *Strange Case of Dr. Jekyll and Mr. Hyde* (1886) is the classical story of the alter ego in Western tradition. Dr. Jekyll experiments with a potion that will separate good from evil in the human psyche and ends up setting his own evil nature free as Mr. Hyde.
- Hans Christian Andersen's short story "The Shadow" (1847) tells of a scholar who loses his shadow, only to be confronted with it later as an individual, a ruthless person who exploits him.
- From Fyodor Dostoyevsky's novel *Crime and Punishment* (1866) two scenes are selected: (1) Raskolnikov dreams about a childhood experience in which he saw a workhorse being beaten to death; (2) Raskolnikov speculates that the extraordinary man is allowed to transgress laws in the name of his greatness.

SOME ADDITIONAL NARRATIVES ILLUSTRATING
THE THEME OF THE ALTER EGO

The Bible, The Old Testament, Genesis: the story of Cain and Abel.

Hans Christian Andersen, "The Marsh King's Daughter," short story (1858).

George Bataille, *L'Abbe C*, novel (1950).

East of Eden, film (1955). A more focused discussion than in the Steinbeck novel, which is more concerned with the power of the will to fight evil.

Star Trek (original television series): "Mirror Mirror" (1967).

Dead Ringers, film (1988).

Star Trek: The Next Generation: several episodes involving Data and his evil twin, Lor, including "Descent I-II" (1993).

Human Nature Is Bad/Human Nature Is Good

- William Golding's novel *Lord of the Flies* (1954) tells of a group of boys stranded on a tropical island while the world is at war; with no adult supervision, only a few boys retain their civilized manners, reasoning, and feelings, while the rest soon revert to a tribalism of territorial aggression and superstition.

SUGGESTION _____

Since your students have by now been exposed to the idea of the alter ego, you may suggest a psychological reading of *Lord of the Flies:* an interpretation of the characters of Piggy and Jack as metaphors for the two forces in Ralph fighting for dominance—two alter egos, each representing a force in human nature.

SOME ADDITIONAL NARRATIVES ILLUSTRATING THE QUESTION OF EVIL HUMAN NATURE

Voltaire's *Candide*, novel (1759).

Samuel Butler, *The Way of All Flesh*, novel (1903).

- The film *Dances with Wolves* (1990) not only illustrates that human nature can be good but ties this view in with the romantic notion introduced by Rousseau that nature is good in itself if left alone. A Civil War soldier is assigned to an outpost during the Indian Wars, but after meeting a Sioux tribe and becoming accepted by them he finds that life with the Indians is more meaningful than life in white civilization.

SOME ADDITIONAL NARRATIVES ILLUSTRATING THE QUESTION OF NATURE AS GOOD IN ITSELF

Hans Christian Andersen, "The Nightingale," short story (1844); "The Bell," short story (1845).

The Roots of Heaven, film (1958).

A Man Called Horse, film (1970).

Never Cry Wolf, film (1983).

The Eternal Return of the Same

- This section explores the possibility of time repeating itself and the consequences for the freedom of the will.

- In Albert Camus's *The Myth of Sisyphus* (1955), the original Greek legend of Sisyphus is outlined and compared with Camus's existentialist version: When we discover that life is absurd, we have only two options—suicide or recovery.
- The first excerpt from Nietzsche's philosophical novel *Thus Spoke Zarathustra* (1892) tells of the gateway of Moment, where everything that has happened will happen again and recur eternally. In the second excerpt, a young shepherd finds that a snake has crawled into his mouth while he was asleep, and he bites its head off, free of the anguish.
- In Ken Grimwood's award-winning science fiction novel *Replay* (1987), a middle-aged man dies and finds himself transported back in time to his college days, but with the memories of his adult life. This time around, can he change history? His life repeats itself over and over again, while he learns a moral lesson.

SOME ADDITIONAL NARRATIVES ILLUSTRATING THE QUESTION OF TIME REPEATING ITSELF AND/OR OTHER NIETZSCHEAN THEMES

Søren Kierkegaard, *Repetition* (1843). Because so few narratives have explored this theme, to my knowledge, I have included this influential, nonfictional work.

Axel Sandemose, *A Fugitive Crosses His Tracks*, novel (1933). Examines the small-town attitude of resentment and prejudice toward artists and other people with talent.

Groundhog Day, film (1993)

THE THEME OF PERSPECTIVISM

The theme of reality being composed of individual perspectives is illustrated by the following stories:

Rashomon, film (1950).

Claude Mauriac, *The Marquise Went Out at Five*, novel (1961).

Philip K. Dick, *Ubik*, novel (1969).

He Said, She Said, film (1991).

Like Water for Chocolate, film (1991).

Some Visions of the Soul and the State

- This section gives a few narrative examples of theories of the human psyche and of the relationship between the person and the state.
- Sophocles' tragedy *Oedipus Rex* tells of King Oedipus who, in his effort to avoid killing his father and marrying his mother, flees to a foreign country where he kills a man and marries a woman; these people turn out to be his birth parents.

- The Hitchcock film *Marnie* (1964) is the story of a young woman who, traumatized by childhood experiences, develops a pattern of theft and fraud; she undergoes a classical psychoanalytic cure with the help of her husband, repeating the childhood experience.

- Kurt Vonnegut's short story "Harrison Bergeron" (1970) tells satirically of a future society where, by decree, everyone is the same, and if someone has a mental or physical advantage over someone else, the person with the advantage is forced to wear "handicapper" items that will neutralize the advantage.

- The film *The Grapes of Wrath* (1940), based on John Steinbeck's book, shows the plight of the have-nots during the 1930s. A family of farmers is forced to leave their ancestral land in the Midwest and become migrant workers in California.

- Ayn Rand's novel *Atlas Shrugged* (1957), which we encountered before in Chapter 7, is used here to illustrate what Rand sees as a story of the failure of communism. Workers of a factory decide to share all profits according to need and work according to ability, and the results are horrible and demeaning: Nobody wants to work, and parasites take advantage of the system.

SOME ADDITIONAL NARRATIVES ILLLUSTRATING FREUDIAN THEORY AND THE DEBATE BETWEEN COMMUNISM AND CAPITALISM

THE SOUL

Psycho, film (1960).

Freud, film (1962). The story of the life of Freud, explored according to psychoanalytical principles.

Murmur of the Heart, film (1971).

The Offense, film (1973).

Iris Murdoch, *The Sacred and Profane Love Machine*, novel (1974). Explores dream symbolism.

Pat Conroy, *The Prince of Tides*, novel (1986) and film (1991).

Most of film director Ingmar Bergman's films.

Most of film director Woody Allen's films.

THE STATE

Ivan Turgenev, *Fathers and Sons*, novel (1862).

Martin Andersen Nexø, *Pelle the Conqueror*, novel (1906–10) and film (1988).

Walk East on Beacon, film (1952).

Boris Pasternak, *Doctor Zhivago*, novel (translated 1958) and film (1965).

Joe Hill, film (1971).

Reds, film (1981).

Martin Cruz Smith, *Gorky Park*, novel (1981) and film (1983).

Business as Usual, film (1987).

The Russia House, film (1990).

The Hunt for Red October, film (1990).

For strictly anticommunist films, you have the entire collection of James Bond novels and films to choose from.

- Ilya Ehrenburg tells of an episode from the occupation of Leningrad, and reflects on the survival value of good books

---

SUGGESTION

Some of your students may know that Ilya Ehrenburg was a communist writer who managed to survive all the major political upheavals in the Soviet Union, including Stalinism. You might consider discussing to what extent a writer's political background should influence our reading of his or her works.

- A final word about stories and morals: A word of encouragement for students to explore stories with a moral significance on their own.

SUGGESTED EXAMINATION FORMATS AND TEST QUESTIONS

This section provides you with some suggestions for the format and material for objective and subjective tests.

I often hand out a sheet of information prior to a test so that the students can familiarize themselves with not only the material but also the format of the test. Such a sheet of information may look like this (reflecting my own preference for test formats):

Format for Multiple-Choice and True/False Tests (objective tests)

Examination Format

Make sure your scantron answers are clear and unambiguous; otherwise, the scantron machine cannot read them. Read the questions carefully. Total possible points: 100. **No books, no notes.**

True/False Questions: (A) = True, (B) = False. 2 points for each correct answer.

Multiple-Choice Questions: 2 points for each correct answer.

Short Answers: Write your answers in the Blue Book, **with a pen.** If you use pencil, you will **lose 5 points.** An excellent answer is worth 5 points, a very good answer gets 4 points; a not-quite-sufficient or too-short answer is worth 3 points, and a poor answer (hardly anything correct) is worth 1 point. A wrong or a blank answer gets 0. Make sure you write the numbers of each question next to your answer. Be as clear, brief, and specific as you can, and please write legibly!

Plagiarism Policy: Using open books or notes during the test, or consulting with other students, will result in an F if discovered.

Format for Essay Tests (subjective tests)

Examination Format

This will be an essay test, and you will need a Blue Book.

The following information will be on the test: Answer one [or more] of the following questions. Please write the number of the question[s] you've chosen on the **front** of your Blue Book. **No notes, no books, no pencils.**

Suggested Approach: (1) Read the questions *carefully* and choose one, (2) "brainstorm," (3) write outline, (4) write essay.

Plagiarism Policy: Using open books or notes during the test, or consulting with other students, will result in an F if discovered.

I tend to give essay questions with a basic structure similar to this (but more detailed):

Answer all parts of this question in the following order:

1. Describe the theory of _____ and illustrate it with examples.
2. Give an account of the criticism of this theory, using arguments from the textbook.
3. Do you agree with the theory? Explain why or why not. You may use arguments of your own.

Format of Term Papers

Format of Term Paper

[Your preferred number of pages, such as 5–8] typed, double-spaced pages. For each quote or reference you must have a footnote or endnote stating author, year, and publisher, even if you are only referring to the textbooks. Any standard reference method will be accepted. The footnotes/endnotes are *in addition to* the required pages (a page of endnotes doesn't qualify as one of the term paper pages).

HOW-TO? A good policy: Express yourself in your own words whenever possible (imagine you are explaining it to a bright friend who has never heard of it before), and save the quotes for very important phrases that you would like to leave the way the author expressed them. Don't "pad" your paper with quotes, and never put a quote in a paper without any explanation. You must follow up and explain why you think the quote is important.

A Word of Caution: Plagiarism will result in a substantial penalty, depending on the severity of the plagiarism. **What is plagiarism in a term paper?** Having someone else write the paper for you. Or copying from someone else's paper. Or copying/quoting from a book or an article without stating your source (without "reference") so that the reader thinks it is your own idea, even if you didn't intend to pass it off as your own. Even if you change a few words here and there it is still considered plagiarism!

In all such handouts before a test or a term paper, I have made it a habit to outline the criterion for plagiarism; in my experience it doesn't happen often that students plagiarize, but you may find it happening under certain circumstances: (1) The student is desperate to get a good grade and is fully aware of transgressing, (2a) the student is genuinely unaware of what constitutes plagiarism, and (2b) the student is from another country and is either used to other rules or has not understood the general rules of

American schools. It is not impossible that you may encounter students from cultures that view plagiarism in a different light; in Western history, plagiarism was not considered an unscientific or unacceptable approach until well into the nineteenth century, and it is conceivable that some foreign students have grown up with a different set of values and are not aware of the severity with which we regard plagiarism today. Giving students the benefit of the doubt, you can avoid misunderstandings such as circumstances 2a and 2b by including a note about plagiarism. There is not much to be done about circumstance number 1 except make the student aware that you will give him or her a failing grade if he or she cheats.

Test Questions

The test questions follow the order of the topics in *The Moral of the Story*; however, for the most effective testing you may want to change the order and test the students on several chapters at a time, mixing up the questions.

On a few occasions I have chosen to insert a bit of humor in the objective test questions; it works well as a diffuser of tension during the test, and I doubt that it misleads the student any more than the other false options do. However, if that doesn't fit your teaching style, you are of course free to skip the "funny" options.

Having received my education within an intellectual tradition where objective tests in the humanities are nonexistent, I have certain reservations about using such tests, and I certainly want to advise against using objective tests *exclusively*, which is why I have included essay questions in each section. These essay questions can also be used as term paper questions.

Grading has been made so much easier by using scantrons, but I suggest always going over the correct answers with the students and not just hand over their test results so that the false options don't get a chance to lodge in their minds forever. For the same reason I find that it is not a good idea to use too many objective questions for a final exam if there is no wrap-up meeting after the final, no matter how convenient such an arrangement may be (because objective questions are easier to grade than essay questions, and we are all pressed for time during finals week).

In Chapters 1, 7, 13, and 20 each narrative outline is followed by study-questions. These questions are also designed for use as essay questions or topics for term paper questions; some of them appear as essay questions in this section.

CHAPTER 1
Who Cares About Ethics?

True/False Questions

1. A misanthropic view of morals is a view that mistrusts the moral capabilities of humans. (T)

2. "Morality" usually refers to theories about the moral rules we follow. (F)

3. The Golden Rule: Do unto others before they do it to you. (F)

4. The Golden Rule: Do unto others as you would have them do unto you. (T)

5. There is common agreement among ethicists that it is not possible for an atheist to have morals. (F)

6. Jürgen Habermas claims that scientific research is not value-free. (T)

7. Not all moral issues are relevant for lawgivers. (T)

8. Frankenstein's monster is an example of a story exploring the problem of research without a conscience. (T)

9. *Altered States* is an example of a story exploring bad business ethics. (F)

10. In *Working Girl*, Tess steals her boss's idea and passes it off as her own. (F)

11. In *Network* a television executive stages acts of terrorism with exclusive rights for the station so that the station can get high ratings. (T)

Multiple-Choice Questions

(Correct answers are marked with an asterisk.)

12. Which one of these answers to the question "Why are there moral rules?" is NOT in Chapter 1?
    a. Moral rules come from God/the gods.
    b. Moral rules originate in human reason.
    *c. Moral rules are dictated by the economy.
    d. Moral rules derive from the fear of being caught.

13. The scientist in *Altered States* experiments on mind expansion by using
    a. a virtual reality headset.
    *b. a sensory deprivation tank.
    c. meditation.
    d. an oxygen tent.

14. What is Katharine's decisive action in *Working Girl?*
    *a. She steals her assistant's idea and passes it off as her own.
    b. She promotes her assistant.
    c. She steals her assistant's boyfriend but refuses to marry him.
    d. She is Tess's assistant and steals her boss's idea.

15. What is the point of the story about the television executive in *Network?*
    a. She is new on the job and doesn't go through channels.
    b. She is reacting to social pressure and decides that she is not going to take it anymore.
    c. She is a terrorist herself.
    *d. She is violating the ethical standards of journalism.

Essay Questions

16. Explain the difference between morals and ethics.
17. Give a critical evaluation of the concept "family values," with examples.
18. Why is it insufficient, according to most theories of ethics, to answer the question of what is morally right or wrong by referring to God's commands?
19. Present a "scruple," and suggest solutions to it.
20. Can science work in a value-free environment, or does science have a duty to work within a system of moral values?
21. Who is the worst moral transgressor in *Working Girl:* Katharine, who steals Tess's idea, or Tess, who lies to make a deal?
22. Would you approve of media censorship under certain circumstances? If no, why not? If yes, when?

CHAPTER 2
Stories in Our Lives

True/False Questions

1. The moral of "The Boy Who Cried Wolf" is that you should never lie, because sooner or later people aren't going to believe you anymore, even when you tell the truth. (T)

2. The lesson of the story of the Little Fir Tree is that one should always save for a rainy day. (F)

3. There is a difference between stories that moralize and stories that discuss moral problems. (T)

4. A didactic story is a story that teaches a lesson. (T)

5. There is a sharp distinction between factual and fictional stories. (F)

6. Even stories that are believed to be factual have an element of poetic creativity. (T)

7. Traditional myths have two purposes: to strengthen social bonding and to serve as wish fulfillment. (F)

8. Fairy tales are, to some psychoanalysts, pure wish fulfillment. (T)

9. In "The Juniper Tree" the girl, Marjory, eats her stepmother and buries her bones under a big tree. (F)

10. The story of the prodigal son belongs to the category of parables. (T)

11. Kierkegaard believes that Abraham's obedience to God was not an example of ordinary morality, but required a leap of faith. (T)

12. We can learn moral lessons from morally good people, but not from morally flawed people. (F)

13. If one is opposed to war, one can find no moral lessons in war stories. (F)

14. The story of the Golem figure teaches a lesson of keeping a moral perspective in our undertakings. (T)

15. In the novel *The Sorrows of Werther*, young Werther kills his beloved Lotte because she has broken up with him. (F)

16. Plato claimed that art is harmful because it fans violent emotions. (T)

17. Aristotle viewed art as dangerous because it fans violent emotions. (F)

18. The story of Dr. Faust has become a metaphor for the scientist who will do anything for knowledge or for gain. (T)

19. The story of Dr. Faust has become a metaphor for the selflessness of doctors. (F)

20. A story of an alter ego is always a story of two selfish persons trading places. (F)

21. Even if a quest is unsuccessful, the search itself lends the searcher a cloak of heroism. (T)

Multiple-Choice Questions

(Correct answers are marked with an asterisk.)

22. The Trobriand people distinguish between three different kinds of stories. Which one does not belong on the list?
    a. sacred stories about the beginning of the world
    b. fairy tales told as entertainment
    c. semihistorical accounts of heroes
    *d. profane stories exaggerating one's personal achievements

23. The moral message of gruesome fairy tales may be the following:
    a. Evil is a continuous presence which we sooner or later fall victim to.
    b. Only evil people have evil things happen to them.
    c. Nothing is so bad that something good doesn't result from it.
    *d. Evil can be dealt with if we have fortitude.

24. What is a parable?
    a. the same as a fairy tale
    *b. an allegorical story for adults
    c. a concept from mathematics, describing a curve
    d. a story with two parallel endings

25. Why did the father of the prodigal son celebrate his homecoming?
    a. He had been away for thirty years.
    b. He brought his new wife with him.
    *c. The father had given him up for lost.
    d. The father was hoping that the son would help around the farm.

26. What is the implicit message of most slasher movies?
    *a. Sex and violent death are connected.
    b. Evil is always vanquished by the good.
    c. Violence is morally wrong, but sex is not.
    d. There is no implicit message in slasher movies.

Essay Questions

27. Relate the Trobriand myth of the grandmother who shed her skin, and analyze its moral message.
28. Relate the story of Abraham and Isaac, and analyze its meaning.
29. Compare Plato's and Aristotle's views on whether art has a positive or a negative influence, and discuss the topic of violence in films and on television with reference to Plato's and Aristotle's theories.
30. Discuss the following statement with examples from film and literature: "Literature can be used to raise one's awareness of potential future moral problems."
31. What is an alter ego?

CHAPTER 3
Ethical Relativism

True/False Questions

1. Some cultures feel that it is their moral duty to dispose of their seniors when they become unproductive. (T)

2. Hard universalism is the theory that we are each entitled to our own moral opinion and that there is no universal moral code. (F)

3. The moral nihilist believes that deep down all people have some values in common. (F)

4. King Darius found that the Callatians would not give up burning their dead, while the Greeks refused to give up eating their dead. (F)

5. Cultural relativism is a normative theory. (F)

6. Cultural relativism describes how customs differ from culture to culture. (T)

7. Ethical relativism is a normative theory. (T)

8. A normative ethical theory involves a moral judgment, evaluation, or justification. (T)

9. Benedict tells of the Northwest Coast Indians that when the chief's sister died, the tribe set out to find the culprits and kill them. (F)

10. Benedict's conclusion is that a certain behavior may be normal for a culture, but that doesn't mean it is morally right. (F)

11. Benedict is saying that morality is culturally defined. (T)

12. If a theory has a breaking point, it should be discarded altogether. (F)

13. Ethical relativism cannot make a claim to tolerance being universally good if all values are culture-relative. (T)

14. One of the arguments against ethical relativism says that the theory cannot distinguish between the actual morality and the professed morality of a culture. (T)

15. Because we can verify that the earth is round, we can also verify which moral viewpoints are better than others. (F)

16. The problem of induction is that induction induces people to think for themselves. (F)

17. One of the universal cultural values suggested by James Rachels is a rule against incest. (F)

18. Inclusive multiculturalism is also sometimes known as multicultural pluralism. (T)

19. Soft universalism claims there are some underlying values all cultures can agree on. (T)

Multiple-Choice Questions

(Correct answers are marked with an asterisk.)

20. One of these answers is not on the list of the four major approaches to the phenomenon of moral differences:
    a. hard universalism.
    b. ethical relativism.
    *c. ethical egoism.
    d. soft universalism.

21. Why is the problem of induction a problem for ethical relativism?
    a. because it induces people to think for themselves
    *b. because we can never know for certain when we have accumulated enough material to make a theory
    c. because we should be using the method of *deduction*, not induction
    d. because very few people understand the problem of induction

22. What is the key issue for Benedict?
    a. Normality is culturally defined.
    b. The concept of the normal is a variant of the concept of the good.
    c. The majority of any group conform to the values of the group; the deviants are few.
    *d. all of the above

23. Which one of these four arguments is not one of the main arguments against ethical relativism?
    a. Ethical relativism forces us to bow to majority rule.
    b. We can neither condemn nor praise other cultures.
    c. It is hard to determine what might constitute a morally autonomous subgroup.
    *d. Ethical relativism is blasphemous, so it should be prohibited.

24. According to Rachels, there are three universal moral standards, disproving ethical relativism. Which one of these doesn't belong on the list?
    a. a prohibition against lying
    b. care of enough infants to keep society going
    *c. a prohibition against incest
    d. a prohibition against murder

25. What is an *ad hominem* argument?
    *a. a logical fallacy claiming that you are right or wrong because of who you are, not because of what you say
    b. a logical fallacy claiming that if $A = B$, then $B = A$
    c. an argument that is valid for only one particular set of circumstances
    d. an argument devised by men, for men, to the exclusion of women

26. Describe the theory of ethical relativism, and illustrate it with an example from the text.

27. Relate the story of King Darius, the Greeks, and the Callatians, and discuss its implications.

28. What is the difference between descriptive and normative ethics? Explain with an example.

29. Describe the argument that we can neither condemn nor praise other cultures, and explain why this is an argument against ethical relativism.

30. Does Rachels think there are any universal cultural standards? If yes, which ones, and why? If no, why not?

31. Compare exclusive multiculturalism with inclusive multiculturalism, and discuss the implications of both forms.

See Chapter 7 for test questions relating to the narratives illustrating ethical relativism and cultural diversity.

CHAPTER 4
Myself or Others?

True/False Questions

1. A psychological egoist is by definition a selfish person. (F)
2. A psychological egoist is a person who believes that everyone is selfish. (T)
3. "Ought implies can" usually means the same as "if there is a will there is a way." (F)
4. Glaucon uses the story of the Ring of Gyges to express his moral disapproval of anyone who gains an advantage by disregarding the interests of others. (F)
5. The story of the Ring of Gyges indicates that humans will take advantage of any situation if they can get away with it. (T)
6. Psychological egoism is the theory that the only proper way to live is to be selfish; in other words, everyone isn't necessarily selfish by nature, but one ought to be selfish. (F)
7. Glaucon claims that if we gave away two invisibility rings, one to a just person and one to an unjust person, the unjust person would take advantage of the ring, but the just person would not. (F)
8. Thomas Hobbes thought that all acts, even acts of pity, could be attributed to a natural tendency toward selfishness. (T)
9. Inuit whale hunters helped free the whales trapped in the ice off the coast of Alaska. (T)
10. Psychological egoism claims that Mother Teresa is at heart a selfish person. (T)
11. Hedonism means pleasure-seeking. (T)
12. A theory must be theoretically falsifiable in order to be philosophically acceptable. (T)
13. If a theory cannot be falsified under any circumstances, it must be true. (F)
14. Abraham Lincoln was a psychological egoist . (T)
15. The fallacy of the suppressed correlative is a way to refute psychological egoism through logic. (T)
16. Ethical egoism is a decent way to be selfish. (F)
17. An ethical egoist is a person believing that everybody is selfish. (F)
18. Individual ethical egoism is the theory that everyone ought to do what I want. (T)
19. Ethical egoism is a consequentialist theory. (T)
20. The word *altruism* means the same as the word *hedonism*. (F)
21. David Hume believes that all humans are selfish at heart. (F)
22. David Hume holds the theory that humans are by nature benevolent. (T)

23. Peter Singer claims that it is to everyone's evolutionary advantage to look after their own interests and disregard the interests of others. (F)

Multiple-Choice Questions

(Correct answers are marked with an asterisk.)

24. Psychological egoism claims that:
    a. most people will act selfishly if they think they can get away with it.
    b. people always ought to act selfishly.
    c. egoists have a psychological problem.
    *d. people always act selfishly.

25. What is Glaucon's point with his hypothesis of the two rings in the text by Plato?
    a. that any man who has two rings ought to give one of them to a needy person
    b. that if we have two invisibility rings and give one to a good man and one to a bad one, the good man will do good deeds with it and the bad man will do bad deeds
    c. that if we have two invisibility rings and give one to a good man and one to a bad one, the good man will do bad deeds and the bad man will do good deeds
    *d. that if we have two invisibility rings and give one to a good man and one to a bad one, the good man and the bad man will both behave selfishly

26. Why do we feel pity toward others, according to Thomas Hobbes?
    a. We are benevolent by nature and feel sympathetic toward others.
    *b. We are afraid their misfortune might happen to us.
    c. We are afraid they will find out that we don't care about their misfortune.
    d. We are stupid. Smart people don't feel pity, according to Hobbes.

27. There are three major reasons for choosing to believe in psychological egoism. Which of the following is not one of them?
    a. the theory appeals to our modern-day cynicism
    b. the theory appeals to our honesty
    *c. the theory allows us to choose when to be selfish and when to consider the feelings of others
    d. the theory serves as an excuse for not trying to do something for others

28. What is the paradox of hedonism?
    a. You can never have too much pleasure.
    b. You cannot love more than one person at the same time.
    c. You must find pleasure in your own company before you can find pleasure in the company of others.
    *d. The harder you look for pleasure, the more it is likely to elude you.

100

29. What is the fallacy of the suppressed correlative?
    a. the same as an *ad hominem* argument
    b. to believe that you can understand yourself by suppressing your memories of your family history
    *c. one way of criticizing psychological egoism: it suppresses the term of unselfishness, which is the correlative of selfishness
    d. to think you can avoid a problem by suppressing it

30. Abraham Lincoln claimed that he saved the pigs from drowning because
    *a. he wouldn't have had peace of mind all day otherwise.
    b. they were his property, and he didn't want to lose the investment.
    c. he wanted to prove that he was a good and kind person.
    d. he liked pigs.

31. Ethical egoism doesn't work in practice because
    a. some people are not willing to be selfish.
    *b. if everybody looks after his or her own self-interests, then you will have a lot of competition.
    c. humans are by nature benevolent.
    d. if you try to look after your own interests, you will be hindered by others who disapprove of ethical egoism.

Essay Questions

32. Give a brief account of the story of the Ring of Gyges. How does Glaucon use it to express a hypothesis of human nature?

33. Would you characterize Lincoln's opinion of his own act of saving the pigs as that of a psychological or an ethical egoist? Your answer should contain a precise definition of both theories.

34. What is the "fallacy of the suppressed correlative"? Use an example to explain.

35. Explain why ethical egoism is not a valid moral theory.

36. Give an account of Singer's argument against ethical egoism.

See Chapter 7 for test questions relating to the narratives illustrating egoism.

CHAPTER 5
Using Your Reason, Part 1: Utilitarianism

True/False Questions

1. The principle of utility is the same as the greatest happiness principle. (T)
2. Any theory concerned with the consequences of actions is a utilitarian theory. (F)
3. For Bentham, moral goodness is the same as pleasure, and moral evil is the same as pain. (T)
4. Bentham's interest in moral theory was primarily theoretical. (F)
5. An instrumental value is something you value for its own sake. (F)
6. Bentham believes that pleasure is an intrinsic value. (T)
7. A value cannot be both intrinsic and instrumental at the same time. (F)
8. The hedonistic calculus is a method by which we calculate the utility of an action according to its ability to produce pleasure or prevent pain. (T)
9. The hedonistic calculus is a method designed primarily to calculate how much pain and pleasure you yourself will get out of a course of action. (F)
10. One of the arguments against the hedonistic calculus is that it promotes selfish interests. (F)
11. One of the arguments against the hedonistic calculus is that it is biased in favor of our choice of values. (T)
12. Mill claims that utilitarianism fails, because we can never make a decision since we cannot calculate all future consequences. (F)
13. For Bentham the criterion for who belongs in the moral universe is who can suffer. (T)
14. Utilitarianism is against any form of animal experiments because experiments cause suffering to the animal. (F)
15. Utilitarianism might allow for using human suffering as a means of entertainment if the happiness produced outweighs the suffering. (T)
16. J. S. Mill claims that it is better to be a pig than to be a fool. (F)
17. The philosopher Epicurus was J. S. Mill's godfather. (F)
18. Mill claims that something is desirable if it is desired. (T)
19. The naturalistic fallacy attempts to make a statement about what is the case based on a statement about what ought to be the case. (F)
20. Mill believed that the government should not interfere with people's lives unless they do harm to themselves. (F)
21. Mill was a champion of women's rights. (T)
22. Mill believed that whole populations could not be trusted to govern themselves because they were not sufficiently mature. (T)

23. Act and rule utilitarianism are one and the same thing. (F)

Multiple-Choice Questions

(Correct answers are marked with an asterisk.)

24. Utilitarianism would agree to which one of the following statements?
    a. It is morally praiseworthy to disregard one's own interests for the sake of other people.
    *b. The end justifies the means.
    c. God determines the ultimate values of good and evil.
    d. Might makes right.

25. Mill disagrees with Bentham by claiming the following:
    a. The principle of utility is the one universal moral principle.
    b. The greatest happiness principle is the one universal moral principle.
    *c. There is a qualitative difference between pleasures.
    d. There is a quantitative difference between pleasures.

26. Utilitarianism may agree to animal experiments under certain circumstances. Which is the most likely circumstance?
    a. any time, because we have no obligations to nonrational creatures
    *b. whenever it is likely to bring about so much happiness or decrease unhappiness to such a degree that it outweighs the suffering of the animal
    c. whenever we can determine that the suffering of the animal is minimal
    d. whenever there is a large amount of happiness at stake in terms of profit for the doctors, the university, or business

27. How does Mill propose to determine which pleasures are higher and which are lower?
    a. by taking a poll in a local region
    b. by selecting answers from people capable of appreciating higher pleasures and having no experience with lower pleasures
    *c. by asking people who have experience with both kinds of pleasure
    d. by reading the newspapers

28. Who wrote, "Capacity for the nobler feelings is in most natures a very tender plant, easily killed, not only by hostile influences, but by mere want of sustenance"?
    a. Bentham
    b. Epicurus
    c. Benedict
    *d. Mill

29. According to J. S. Mill, there is only one legitimate reason for interfering with other people's lives:
   *a. if they do harm to others.
   b. if they do harm to themselves.
   c. if you possess relevant knowledge about their welfare that is unavailable to them.
   d. Trick question: Mill thought there were NO legitimate reasons to interfere with other people's lives.

30. What is act utilitarianism?
   a. the same as rule utilitarianism: the consequences of any type of act (rule) are what count
   *b. the same as Bentham's utilitarianism: the consequences of any single act are what count
   c. the opposite of passive utilitarianism
   d. the part of utilitarianism which allows you to think of yourself only

Essay Questions

31. What is the "hedonistic calculus"? Explain, and give an example of how to use it.

32. According to Mill, how can we make a decision without knowing the consequences? Explain and discuss.

33. What is the harm principle? Explain with an example.

34. Describe the difference between act utilitarianism and rule utilitarianism.

35. How would a utilitarian respond to the suggestion that alien beings would be allowed to abduct involuntary human subjects for lethal medical experiments provided that they give humanity a cure for all viral diseases, including AIDS? Evaluate the answer from the standpoint of an act utilitarian and a rule utilitarian.

36. Evaluate the following statement from a utilitarian point of view: "Tests are causing suffering to students, and professors always complain about having to grade tests, so tests should be abolished."

See Chapter 7 for test questions relating to the narratives illustrating utilitarianism and Kant's deontology.

CHAPTER 6
Using Your Reason, Part 2: Kant's Deontology

True/False Questions

1. In Kant's moral theory, we use our maxim primarily to maximize the happiness of everyone involved. (F)

2. In Kant's view, a good will cannot be good if it doesn't take consequences of one's actions into account. (F)

3. In Kant's view, a good will is good regardless of whether it accomplishes its purpose or not. (T)

4. Kant is a hard universalist. (T)

5. The hypothetical imperative is a conditional command, describing an "if-then" situation. (T)

6. According to Kant, an act that is done for other reasons than a sense of duty is not necessarily a morally wrong act. (T)

7. A maxim is an act that has a maximum amount of good consequences. (F)

8. Universalization means to ask yourself if everyone actually agrees with your own moral values. (F)

9. When we universalize a maxim, we ask ourselves if it could be made into a universal law. (T)

10. To be an autonomous lawmaker means that you are a member of the government and you cannot be bribed. (F)

11. Kant has been criticized for claiming that his theory does not take consequences into account, when in fact it does. (T)

12. Among the criticisms raised against Kant's categorical imperative is the following: The categorical imperative discriminates against people of no or low income. (F)

13. According to Kant, a rational being is any being capable of feeling pleasure or pain. (F)

14. Being used as merely a means to an end is the same as being regarded as having instrumental value only. (T)

15. Being treated as a means to an end is the same as being used merely as a means. (F)

16. Rational beings have intrinsic value according to Kant. (T)

17. Rebecca, a college student, is being used merely as a means to an end by her college professors because they get paid for teaching classes, and without Rebecca and other students they would not receive a paycheck. (F)

18. Kant thinks that we can treat animals any way we like, including being cruel to them. (F)

19. Humans who don't qualify as rational beings must, according to Kant's own theory, be classified as things. (T)

20. "Kingdom of Ends" refers to Kant's theory of history: When everyone has learned to use the categorical imperative, history will come to an end. (F)

Multiple-Choice Questions

(Correct answers are marked with an asterisk.)

21. What is a deontological theory?
    a. a theory about proper dental care
    b. a theory assessing the overall consequences of an action
    c. the same as a consequentialist theory
    *d. a theory assessing the morality of an action in terms of duty or rightness in itself

22. A store owner is trying to decide whether or not to cheat her customers. Which one of her arguments would qualify as a moral decision, according to Kant?
    a. She decides to try to cheat her customers on occasion when she is certain she can get away with it.
    b. She decides not to cheat her customers because it would not be prudent: She might be found out and lose all her customers.
    *c. She decides not to cheat her customers because such an act could not be made into a universal law.
    d. She decides not to cheat her customers because she likes them very much.

23. What is an autonomous lawmaker?
    a. a member of the government who cannot be bribed
    b. someone who is capable of influencing the legislation in his or her own favor
    *c. a person who follows the categorical imperative
    d. a person who follows hypothetical imperatives

24. Which one of the following is not a major criticism raised against Kant's moral theory?
    *a. The categorical imperative discriminates against people of no or low income.
    b. There is a loophole in the categorical imperative: A situation can be described so it doesn't apply.
    c. The categorical imperative doesn't allow for exceptions.
    d. The view of what is rational depends on who holds the view.

25. Kant has three main themes in his book *Grounding*. Which one of the following does not belong?
    a. the theory that people should be treated as ends in themselves
    *b. the theory about the inalienable right to the pursuit of happiness for rational beings
    c. the theory of the categorical imperative
    d. the theory of people forming a moral community, the Kingdom of Ends

26. What does Kant mean by "universal law"?
    a. a law of physics, like gravity
    b. a moral law dictated by a moral authority
    *c. a moral law, binding for all rational beings
    d. a civic law, binding for all citizens

Essay Questions

27. What is "universalization"? Explain, and give an example.

28. What is a hypothetical imperative? Explain in detail, and give an example.

29. What is a categorical imperative? Explain in detail, and give an example.

30. Evaluate the following statement: "Actions are only morally good if they are done because of a good will." Explain "good will," and give reasons why you think the statement is correct or incorrect.

31. Imagine a chimpanzee, Kiki, in a university lab. Imagine that the research program is being canceled and that Kiki is now scheduled for "termination." Evaluate the situation from a utilitarian viewpoint and from a Kantian viewpoint. Do you have a solution?

32. Analyze the following statement: "Act in such a way that you treat humanity, whether in your own person or in the person of another, always at the same time as an end and never simply as a means."

33. What is the Kingdom of Ends?

See Chapter 7 for test questions relating to the narratives illustrating utilitarianism and Kant's deontology.

CHAPTER 7
Narratives of Right and Wrong Conduct

True/False Questions

1. In *Do the Right Thing*, Mookie's life is saved by a black police officer. (F)
2. In *Do the Right Thing*, the Korean store owner claims to be black. (T)
3. In *The Last of the Mohicans*, Cora falls in love with the Huron Indian Magua. (F)
4. The lesson taught in the film *The Last of the Mohicans* is that there can be no understanding between whites and Native Americans. (F)
5. In *A Passage to India*, Dr. Aziz is an Indian professor of philosophy. (F)
6. In *A Passage to India*, Adele withdraws all her accusations of assault. (T)
7. The character of Lawrence in *Lawrence of Arabia* is purely fictional. (T)
8. The Arab warriors tell Lawrence that they believe that every man makes his own destiny: Nothing is determined beforehand. (F)
9. In *Sideshow*, a small child is being sent downriver to his death, and nobody interferes because each country has a right to do things their own way. (T)
10. In *Sideshow*, the planet Elsewhere consists of a number of countries pledged to the concept of cultural diversity. (T)
11. Emma Bovary kills herself because her lover has left her. (F)
12. Scarlett O'Hara (*Gone with the Wind*) undergoes a crisis of conscience after killing her husband, Rhett Butler. (F)
13. *Atlas Shrugged* can be seen as an argument for accepting altruism as the only acceptable ethical theory. (F)
14. In "The Blacksmith and the Baker," an innocent baker is being executed for the crime of the blacksmith. (T)
15. In *The Brothers Karamazov*, Alyosha would not consent to the torture of a small creature for the sake of human happiness. (T)
16. In "The Ones Who Walk Away from Omelas," the happiness of the community is based on a dog being tortured. (F)
17. In *Abandon Ship!*, Captain Holmes is concerned primarily with saving his own life. (F)
18. In *Rebel Without a Cause*, Jim challenges the local gang leader to a "chickie-run." (F)
19. In *High Noon*, nobody is willing to help Kane because he has "cried wolf" once too often. (F)
20. In *Star Trek: The Next Generation*: "Justice," Wesley is about to be executed for trespassing. (T)

(Correct answers are marked with an asterisk.)

21. In the novel *Sideshow*, a child killer has been apprehended by an Enforcer. What is the Enforcer's reason for catching him?
    a. because he is a criminal: he has killed a child
    b. because he is a danger to the community
    *c. because he took children across borders, interfering in other provinces' affairs
    d. because he killed the Enforcer's own child

22. Why did Emma Bovary take her own life?
    a. because she was terminally ill
    b. because her lover had left her
    *c. because she had sold all her own and her husband's assets to pay off her debt
    d. because her daughter had found out that she had been seeing another man and threatened to tell Charles Bovary

23. In *Atlas Shrugged*, Ayn Rand's main concern was:
    a. to make people understand that it is everybody's responsibility to make certain that no one goes hungry in this world.
    b. to make people understand utilitarianism.
    *c. to make people understand that it is everyone's right to protect himself or herself from being used by others who want something for nothing.
    d. to make people understand that the Bible is always right.

24. Identify the source of this quote: "You had to act on your own judgment, you had to have the capacity to judge, the courage to stand on the verdict of your mind, and the purest, the most ruthless consecration to the rule of doing right, of doing the best, the utmost best possible to you."
    a. Sheri Tepper, *Sideshow*
    *b. Ayn Rand, *Atlas Shrugged*
    c. Johan Wessel, "The Blacksmith and the Baker"
    d. a quoted line from the film *Do the Right Thing*

25. In "The Blacksmith and the Baker," the judge pronounces a sentence. What is his justification?
    a. The baker is guilty and must be punished.
    b. The townspeople have bribed him to let the blacksmith go.
    c. The blacksmith must be punished for his crime, and nobody can take his place.
    *d. The baker can be punished even if he is innocent, because he is expendable, but the blacksmith is not.

26. In the film *Abandon Ship!*, Captain Holmes put several survivors over the side of the lifeboat. Why?
    a. He was afraid they would gang up on him and kill him.
   *b. He was trying to save the lives of the strongest survivors.
    c. He was trying to save the lives of the weakest survivors.
    d. He was mainly trying to save his own life.

27. In *Rebel Without a Cause*, Jim's father tries to give him advice. Which of the following theories of ethics does his father seem to subscribe to?
    a. a Kantian deontological theory
    b. a theory of psychological egoism
    c. a theory of ethical relativism
   *d. a theory of utilitarianism

28. In *Star Trek: The Next Generation*: "Justice," Picard stops Wesley's execution by presenting an argument that is acceptable to the planet's rulers. What is his argument?
    a. Wesley is underage and cannot be held responsible.
    b. Nobody can be held responsible for not knowing the laws of a foreign culture.
   *c. A moral law is not mature if it does not allow for exceptions.
    d. An appeal to ethical relativism: A moral law of one culture should not be binding on members of another.

Essay Questions

29. Evaluate the riot scene in *Do the Right Thing*: Is there a justification for it? Explain why or why not.

30. Evaluate *Do the Right Thing* as a comment on multiculturalism. Does it support inclusive or exclusive multiculturalism?

31. In *Lawrence of Arabia*, we hear of the Arab and the British view of destiny. Explain and comment on both.

32. Is *Sideshow* an argument for or against ethical relativism? Explain.

33. Is Emma Bovary an egoist? Are we all like Emma, deep down?

34. If Emma Bovary got her ideas about romantic passion from books, does it mean that fiction can be morally dangerous?

35. Compare the characters of Emma Bovary and Scarlett O'Hara: Do they have anything in common? Are there differences between them? Which of the two comes out as more morally tainted?

36. What is the point of "The Ones Who Walk Away from Omelas"? Do you agree with the author? Why or why not?

37. Evaluate the story of the torture in *The Brothers Karamazov* and "The Ones Who Walk Away from Omelas" from a utilitarian and a Kantian point of view.

110

38. Evaluate Captain Holmes's course of action (*Abandon Ship!*) from a utilitarian point of view and a Kantian point of view. Do you believe he was guilty of murder? Why or why not?

39. How can the conflict between Jim and his father in *Rebel Without a Cause* be seen as a conflict between utilitarianism and Kantianism?

40. What makes *High Noon* a Kantian Western?

CHAPTER 8
Socrates, Plato, and the Good Life

True/False Questions

1. Virtue ethics is commonly opposed to ethics of character. (F)
2. Hypatia was a woman philosopher in Egypt. (T)
3. Hypatia was murdered by a mob of fanatical Christian monks. (T)
4. Socrates reportedly claimed that "an unlived life is not worth examining." (F)
5. The Socratic method is also known as a dialectic method. (T)
6. Socrates was primarily interested in teaching the sons and daughters of the Athenian working population. (F)
7. Socrates implied that he was not bound to any one conception of reality unless it could be tested by reason. (T)
8. Socrates was executed by beheading on the final day of the Olympic games. (F)
9. Crito tries to make Socrates agree to attempt to escape because he has been convicted by unjust laws. (T)
10. Plato gathered Socrates's writings and published them under his own name. (F)
11. In his later dialogues, Plato uses the character of Socrates as a mouthpiece for his own philosophy. (T)
12. Socrates believes there is a difference between opinion and knowledge. (T)
13. Both Socrates and Plato were engaged in a life-long intellectual battle in favor of the concept of ethical relativism. (F)
14. In Plato's dialogue *The Republic*, Socrates insists that only a well-balanced person with a sense of justice can be happy. (T)
15. Metaphysics asks questions about the nature of reality. (T)
16. Most philosophers who are interested in metaphysics are also believers in reincarnation. (F)
17. A metaphysical materialist is primarily interested in accumulating material goods. (F)
18. The world of Forms is unchangeable, according to Plato. (T)
19. The Forms are embedded in the world of things, according to Plato. (F)
20. In the "Myth of the Cave," the prisoners symbolize all people who are tied down by a sense of guilt. (F)
21. In the "Myth of the Cave," the prisoners symbolize all humans who think the world of the senses is the real world. (T)

Multiple-Choice Questions

(Correct answers are marked with an asterisk.)

22. Socrates gave several reasons why he did not want to attempt to escape from prison. Which one of these is the most likely one?
    a. because he believed that his sentence was just
    b. because he thought he could make a greater political impact by dying as a martyr
    c. because he was sick and was not able to stand up
    *d. because two wrongs wouldn't make a right

23. Why do people do morally wrong acts, according to Socrates?
    a. because human nature is evil
    *b. because people are ignorant
    c. because they haven't thought to ask themselves, "Could I want this to be a universal law?"
    d. because they haven't considered the consequences

24. A virtuous person must, according to Plato, be able to maintain a balance between the three parts of his or her psyche. Identify the one part that doesn't belong.
    *a. memory
    b. willpower
    c. appetites
    d. reason

25. There are three major theories of metaphysics; identify the one that doesn't belong.
    a. materialism
    *b. realism
    c. idealism
    d. dualism

26. How do we learn about the Forms, according to Plato?
    a. by doing as much empirical research as possible
    b. by examining our emotions
    *c. by using our reason to recall the knowledge we had before we were born
    d. by reading the works of great philosophers

Essay Questions

27. In your opinion, should Socrates have tried to escape? Why or why not?

28. Explain Plato's Theory of Forms by using an example.

29. Explain the difference between materialism, idealism, and dualism, by using examples.

30. Tell the story of the Cave, and explain its philosophical significance.

CHAPTER 9
Aristotle's Virtue Theory

True/False Questions

1. Aristotle was one of Socrates's most brilliant students. (F)
2. For Aristotle the Forms have no existence outside the world of things. (T)
3. The concept of teleology means a theory about the nature of God. (F)
4. According to Aristotle, everything has a function in the order of things, except fleas and snakes. (F)
5. We determine what a thing's purpose is by investigating what the thing in question does best. (T)
6. According to a teleological explanation, giraffes have long necks because of natural selection and mutation. (F)
7. According to a teleological explanation, giraffes have long necks so that they can reach high branches. (T)
8. To Aristotle, virtue means acting with excellence. (T)
9. Aristotle's virtue theory says that there are three kinds of virtue: one which is in deficiency, one which is just right, and one which is in excess. (F)
10. For Aristotle we are morally good if we are capable of choosing the mean between extremes. (T)
11. Every action and emotion has a mean, a deficiency, and an excess. (F)
12. The virtue called proper pride has as its deficiency the vice humility and as its excess the vice prodigality. (F)
13. There is a discrepancy between Aristotle's list of virtues and vices and the Catholic list of cardinal virtues and sins. (T)
14. For Aristotle, true happiness is to be found in contemplation. (T)
15. The Catholic philosopher Saint Augustine relied greatly on the ideas of Aristotle. (F)
16. For Christian ethics, the moral rightness of following God's laws became more important than the belief in the human ability to shape one's own character. (T)
17. Aristotle was accused of the same crime as Socrates. (T)
18. For Aristotle, some virtues are closer to one extreme than the other. (T)
19. Christian scholars kept studying the works of Aristotle until he was rediscovered by Arab thinkers. (F)
20. Today the assumption that everything has a purpose is commonly accepted. (F)

Multiple-Choice Questions

(Correct answers are marked with an asterisk.)

21. Aristotle's theory of causation includes four causes; identify the one that doesn't belong on the list.
    a. the material cause
    b. the final cause
    c. the formal cause
    *d. the ideal cause

22. According to Aristotle, if you have a deficiency of truthfulness, you are
    a. lying.
    b. being rude.
    c. virtuous.
    *d. being ironical.

23. What is teleology?
    a. a theory about the nature of God
    *b. a theory that everything has a purpose
    c. a theory about the technology of broadcasting
    d. another word for *telemetry*

Essay Questions

24. Explain Aristotle's theory of virtues, in detail, using at least three examples. At least two of the examples must be Aristotle's.

25. Explain the difference between a teleological explanation and a causal explanation by using examples.

26. Give an example of a virtue that is closer to one extreme than the other.

27. Evaluate Aristotle's idea that rationality is the overriding human purpose.

28. Describe your own criterion for moral goodness, and give an example of what *you* think is a morally good person. You may make up an example, or pick an actual or fictional person and describe him/her.

See Chapter 13 for test questions relating to the narratives illustrating virtue theory.

CHAPTER 10
Virtues and Values of Other Traditions

True/False Questions

1. Confucius defines the man of virtue as someone wise, courageous, and with a good head for business. (F)
2. The Way is practiced by developing good habits and continual good thinking. (T)
3. Both Aristotle and Confucius believed that it is virtuous to practice moderation. (T)
4. Both Aristotle and Confucius believed in the Golden Rule as the essential moral approach to life. (F)
5. Mencius believed that humans are born morally neutral but are capable of developing toward being either morally good or evil. (F)
6. Mencius believed that in order to become truly virtuous you have to go through suffering. (T)
7. Taoism is a philosophy which advocates that the superior person must try to affect change in order to make life better for others. (F)
8. The concept of *wu-wei* is Taoism's concept for proper conduct: doing nothing. (T)
9. In Buddhism there are numerous Buddhas. (T)
10. Buddhism advocates a renunciation of self-indulgence by way of asceticism and strict self-denial. (F)
11. The concept of karma is a system of reward and punishment for the soul after death. (F)
12. In Buddhism, karma is the force that binds the soul to a new reincarnation because of the accumulated results of past deeds and cravings. (T)
13. Plato has been highly influential in Islamic philosophy. (F)
14. The ideas of fatalism and the idea of free will are mutually supportive philosophies in Islam. (F)
15. In Islam, the true sin is disobedience toward Allah in the sense of forgetting His commands. (T)
16. According to Avicenna, woman's nature is weak and she must be protected from herself so that she will not cause dishonor to her husband. (T)
17. The Jewish rule of charity is directed exclusively toward one's coreligionists. (F)
18. Maimonides advocated that rebellious sons should be put to death. (T)
19. The Viking values include the following: justice among equals, loyalty among family and friends, and mercy and generosity toward strangers and enemies. (F)
20. The Akan people of Ghana believe humans can acquire a good character through listening to stories. (T)
21. The Native American values include an understanding that humans have only a small part to play in the general order of things. (T)

(Correct answers are marked with an asterisk.)

22. Confucius identifies a man of virtue as someone with the following three characteristics. Which of the following is not one of those characteristics?
    a. wisdom
    *b. a good head for business
    c. courage
    d. humaneness

23. Which view is Mencius' own view of human nature?
    a. There is no such thing as human nature.
    b. There are those who are good by nature, and there are those who are evil by nature, but proper guidance can set anybody straight.
    *c. Human nature is good from the beginning, and will remain good if guided right.
    d. Human nature is morally neutral from birth, and it can become good or bad.

24. What is the most important duty, according to Mencius?
    a. the duty toward one's children
    b. the duty toward the state
    *c. the duty toward one's parents
    d. the duty toward one's spouse

25. Gautama received three jolts to his complacency that were to change his life and cause him to found the philosophy of Buddhism. Which of the following is not one of those jolting experiences?
    a. the experience of age
    b. the experience of death
    c. the experience of disease
    *d. the experience of poverty

26. Which of the following is not one of the Four Noble Truths that Buddhism is based on?
    a. Suffering is caused by craving.
    *b. The way to stop life is to meditate on one's cravings.
    c. If cravings stop, suffering will stop, too.
    d. Life is suffering.

27. Maimonides sees four levels of personal growth. Identify the highest level.
    a. the level of everyday life and material possessions
    b. the level of moral virtue, developed by good habits
    c. the level of physical fitness, good health, and an even temper
    *d. the level of rational virtue, developed by understanding God

28. Which tradition expresses these ethical rules: "Be considerate of the feelings of a poor man, by giving him alms in secret, and on no account before others. For this reason also give him food and drink in your own house—but do not watch him while he is eating"?
    a. the Chinese tradition
    *b. the Jewish tradition
    c. the Viking tradition
    d. the Islamic tradition

29. Which tradition expresses this saying: "The road to an enemy is a long detour even if he lives nearby, but the road to a friend is always a shortcut even if he is far away"?
    *a. the Viking tradition
    b. the Jewish tradition
    c. the Chinese tradition
    d. the Islamic tradition

30. The Akan people's view of human nature is
    a. that people are born intrinsically good and become corrupted by bad influence.
    *b. that people are born morally neutral and become good by developing good habits.
    c. that people are born intrinsically evil and must be redeemed through their religious belief.
    d. that some are born good and some are born evil, as a matter of fate.

Essay Questions

31. For those who believe in God's omniscience there is a problem reconciling this idea with the idea of human free will. Explain the problem.
32. Discuss the fundamentalist Islamic custom of protecting women from the world as well as from themselves by keeping them in seclusion.
33. Discuss the saying from *Havamal*: "Cattle die, kindred die, you yourself will die. What never dies is the good name you have won for yourself." Do you agree? Can such a saying apply to our own age?
34. Evaluate the environmentalist values of Native American philosophy. Can they be used in the world of today? Why or why not?

See Chapter 13 for test questions relating to the narratives illustrating non-Western/non-contemporary values.

CHAPTER 11
The Modern Perspective

True/False Questions

1. Virtue ethics claims that we are not responsible for the character and dispositions we are born with. (F)
2. There is a difference between a morality of virtue and an ethics of virtue. (T)
3. Virtue ethics believes that a negative role model cannot teach us anything about virtues; only a positive role model can. (F)
4. Bernard Mayo believes that a virtuous person usually does the right thing, but someone who follows moral rules of conduct may not always be a virtuous person. (T)
5. Kant believed that we learn virtue best from positive role models. (F)
6. Kant insisted that trying to learn virtue from role models does not lead to virtue, but to jealousy and resentment. (T)
7. Philippa Foot stresses that having a virtue is not the same as having a skill; it is having the proper intention. (T)
8. Foot claims that someone who is able to overcome his or her bad inclinations is a morally better person than someone who doesn't have bad inclinations. (F)
9. Christina Hoff Sommers believes that the proper way to teach values is to focus on Christian values of obedience and sexual abstinence. (F)
10. Sommers wants to teach students that values are not merely a matter of taste. (T)
11. Sommers believes that, in the end, moral problems such as pollution, the homeless, or the loneliness of elderly people must be solved by the state and not the individual. (F)
12. Søren Kierkegaard's father believed there was a curse on the family because he, as a child, had stepped on a loaf of bread to get across a mud puddle. (F)
13. Within the Lutheran tradition there is no confession and no absolution of sins by clergy. (T)
14. Kierkegaard shocked Romantic nineteenth-century Europe by claiming, a century ahead of his time, that "objectivity is truth." (F)
15. The character of Judge William is Kierkegaard's symbol of a person who is locked in the aesthetic stage. (F)
16. Heidegger calls humans "Being-There," because human existence is different than the existence of things and animals. (T)
17. Heidegger believes we ought to take into account what "they say," because forgetting about public opinion removes us from total existential awareness. (F)
18. Heidegger thinks humans feel anguish when they realize that all their concerns and rules are relative. (T)
19. Henri Bergson believes our true self will cause us to do unexpected things, but as long as we remain true to ourselves, we can't act in a morally wrong way. (F)

20. Bergson died from pneumonia caused by standing in line during the Nazi occupation of Paris to be registered as a Jew. (T)

21. Sartre's example of the young woman on a date is an example of Bad Faith. (T)

22. For Sartre all your choices count equally, even those you intended to make but never carried out. (F)

23. For Erik Erikson a person with ego integrity is one who has never experienced an identity crisis. (F)

Multiple-Choice Questions

(Correct answers are marked with an asterisk.)

24. For Kierkegaard the phrase "subjectivity is truth" means the following:
    a. There is no objective knowledge, except for mathematical theorems.
    b. There is no objective knowledge, including mathematical theorems.
    *c. There is no objective truth about life, only a personal truth for each individual.
    d. Trick question: Kierkegaard says, "Objectivity is truth," and in this he is in agreement with most of the philosophical tradition.

25. Kierkegaard theorizes that there are three stages to the development of one's character. Which of the following is not one of the stages?
    a. the ethical stage
    *b. the existential stage
    c. the aesthetic stage
    d. the religious stage

26. For Sartre, the belief that there is no God, and life is absurd, leads to the following conclusion:
    *a. Humans must create their own values through making choices.
    b. Everything is permissible, since there will be no eternal punishment.
    c. Since nothing has value, the life of the individual is worthless and human rights are nonexistent.
    d. There is no free will, since all of reality is a matter of material causes and effects.

27. What does Sartre mean by "Bad Faith"?
    a. when you are a bad Catholic
    b. when you trust in someone who turns out to be untrustworthy
    *c. when you try to avoid making a choice by pretending that you have no choice
    d. when you try to pretend that there is no god, but in your heart you really believe God exists

28. Someone who has ego integrity is
    a. someone who has never undergone an identity crisis.
    b. someone who can be trusted in all business ventures.
    *c. someone who has an inner harmony and balance of the mind.
    d. someone who is proud of the fact that he or she cannot be bribed under any circumstances.

Essay Questions

29. Explain the relationship between Kierkegaard and his father, and the consequences it seems to have had for his philosophy.
30. What does Sartre mean by anguish? Explain, and give an example of how it feels and why it happens.
31. What does Sartre mean by saying we are condemned to be free?
32. Explain Sartre's concept of Bad Faith by using two examples: one of Sartre's and one of your own.

See Chapter 13 for test questions relating to the narratives illustrating existentialism and the subject of authenticity.

CHAPTER 12
Case Studies in Virtue

True/False Questions

1. Thomas Hobbes and Jean-Jacques Rousseau agreed that humans are naturally compassionate toward each other. (F)

2. Mencius and Rousseau agreed that humans are good by nature but have been corrupted by the circumstances of life. (T)

3. For Philip Hallie, institutionalized cruelty has the psychological effect that the victim comes to believe the cruelty is justified. (T)

4. Hallie believes that the best antidote against institutionalized cruelty is to show kindness to the victim. (F)

5. Hallie believes that it is better to have compassion, even if you cause death and destruction, than not to have any compassion at all. (F)

6. For Richard Taylor reason has no role to play in moral matters; all one needs is compassion. (T)

7. Taylor's three stories of atrocities show that what counts are the dreadful consequences of these acts, not the intentions behind them. (F)

8. In *Huckleberry Finn*, Huck helps the runaway slave Jim, and Jonathan Bennett thinks Huck is doing the wrong thing. (F)

9. Nobody can demand gratitude from us because gratitude is a feeling we cannot control. (F)

10. Lin Yutang's main point is criticizing the West for being indifferent toward our children and homeless people. (F)

11. Lin Yutang believes we owe a debt of gratitude to our parents for having raised us. (T)

12. Jane English uses the "debt-metaphor" to advocate the idea that grown children owe a debt to their parents for raising them. (F)

13. There are appropriate ways of using the debt-metaphor, according to English, and describing favors between strangers is one of them. (T)

14. For English there are only duties when there are favors, but there are no duties or obligations between friends. (F)

15. Fred Berger believes that in order to determine the amount of gratitude one ought to show, one must look at the giver's intentions. (T)

16. English believes that all dating problems would be solved if both parties would agree at the outset that the date is, basically, a business agreement. (F)

(Correct answers are marked with an asterisk.)

17. What is institutionalized cruelty, according to Philip Hallie?
    a. cruelty committed by personnel in institutions such as boarding schools, orphanages, nursing homes, and hospitals
    *b. a systematic physical and psychological breakdown of victims by victimizers
    c. a systematic physical and psychological breakdown of an individual by members of an institution such as a school or a military academy
    d. cruelty elevated to an art where the physical signs are invisible

18. Imagine you come across a seven-year-old child torturing a puppy. There are several possible arguments you might use that are aimed at dissuading someone from hurting someone else. Which one might Taylor advocate?
    *a. Appeal to his or her compassion: "How do you think the puppy feels?"
    b. Appeal to his or her sense of universalizability: "What if everyone acted like you?"
    c. Appeal to his or her sense of consequences: "You won't get away with it, you know!"
    d. Appeals are a waste of time. Call the police, and in the meantime restrain the kid, not too gently.

19. What is Bennett's argument against Huck Finn?
    a. It was wrong of Huck to help a slave escape because in his day and age slaves were property, and ethical relativism dictates that one must follow the rules of one's society.
    *b. Huck did the right thing, but for the wrong reason: He should have found good reasons for helping Jim rather than just follow his instinct.
    c. Huck did the wrong thing, because he should have pleaded with Jim's owner to free him and not take matters into his own hands.
    d. Huck did the right thing, and Bennett doesn't argue against him at all—trick question.

20. According to Jane English, what kind of obligations do we have toward our parents?
    a. We have no obligations at all, because we didn't ask to be born.
    b. We have an obligation to love them, even if they haven't shown us love.
    c. We have unending obligations, because we owe them everything, since they raised us.
    *d. We have obligations according to their need and our ability to help, as long as there is friendship.

Essay Questions

21. Define Hallie's concept of institutionalized cruelty: (1) What kind of cruelty is it? (2) Why does it happen? and (3) What is the antidote?

22. What is Taylor trying to say with his stories of malice and goodness? Explain by referring to the stories.

23. What is the difference between reciprocity and mutuality in English's theory? Explain with examples.

24. Discuss the issue of dating: a favor-debt situation or a friendship situation? Is there a way to resolve the problem of different expectations for dating partners in the future?

See Chapter 13 for test questions relating to the narratives illustrating the virtue of compassion and other virtues and vices.

CHAPTER 13
Narratives of Virtue and Vice

True/False Questions

1. In *Lord Jim*, Jim abandons ship with the rest of the crew during a storm, causing the death of hundreds of pilgrims. (F)

2. In *Njal's Saga*, Njal's wife and grandson choose to stay with him and be burned alive. (T)

3. In *Njal's Saga*, the little boy Thord is rescued at the last minute by Flosi's son. (F)

4. In *The Seven Samurai*, a group of samurai warriors descend on a village in order to plunder it, but the courage of the villagers drives them away. (F)

5. The parable of the Good Samaritan was told to teach several lessons; one was that Samaritans are people, too. (T)

6. Ivanhoe, son of the Jew Isaac, comes home to his father's house and rescues him from a nightly ambush, thus earning his father's gratitude. (F)

7. In *Othello*, Othello is jealous of his wife because he suspects her of having an affair with his friend Cassio. (T)

8. The moral lesson of *Othello* is that women cannot be trusted: They are by nature promiscuous. (F)

9. In "The Faithful Wife and the Woman Warrior," Blue Hawk's wife has an affair with Red Hawk, and in anger Blue Hawk drowns her in the river. (F)

10. In *Fatal Attraction*, Dan has a brief affair with his wife's sister, Alex. (F)

11. There is no difference between revenge and retribution. (F)

12. Edmond Dantes, the Count of Monte Cristo, is bent on revenge until he realizes that no man should assume that he is the hand of God. (T)

13. Captain Ahab hunts the white whale Moby Dick because he is obsessed with revenge. (T)

14. In *The Searchers*, Ethan eventually kills Debbie because he finds that she has been contaminated by living with the Comanche Indians. (F)

15. The drama *No Exit* features three people on Death Row awaiting their execution. (F)

16. In *No Exit*, Sartre claims that "Hell is other people." (T)

17. In *Hannah and Her Sisters*, Mickey almost kills himself and recaptures the meaning of life as a consequence. (T)

18. The little boy Åke is plunged into anguish when he envisions himself becoming a cockroach. (F)

19. Babette spends her entire inheritance on cooking an elaborate meal for the congregation of the small village that took her in as a refugee. (T)

20. In *Star Wars*, the Dark Side of the Force seems good and right to those who have chosen it. (T)

21. In *The Good Apprentice*, Edward is filled with guilt because he has caused the death of one of his friends. (T)

Multiple-Choice Questions

(Correct answers are marked with an asterisk.)

22. Why is Othello jealous of his wife, Desdemona?
    *a. His enemy, Iago, has hinted that she is having an affair.
    b. His enemy, Iago, is having an affair with her.
    c. He is jealous of everyone she has known before she met him, including Iago.
    d. She is having an affair with his friend Cassio.

23. The hypochondriac in *Hannah and Her Sisters* has a severe case of existential angst (anguish). Why?
    a. He is afraid that he cannot pay the doctor's bill.
    b. He is afraid that he might have AIDS.
    *c. He thinks life is meaningless since everybody must die.
    d. He thinks God will punish him by sending him to Hell.

24. Which of the following is one of the points Sartre makes in *No Exit*?
    a. to show the anguish of people on Death Row awaiting their execution
    b. to show the terrors of Hell so that his readers can become good Catholics and avoid bad faith
    *c. to show that only the deeds we have actually done count for something, and not our unfulfilled plans
    d. to show that all humans are benevolent by nature

25. In *The Good Apprentice*, Edward finally emerges as
    a. a callous, insensitive clod.
    *b. a moral catalyst for his surroundings.
    c. a murderer.
    d. a priest who is finally able to forgive himself.

Essay Questions

26. Is Jim *(Lord Jim)* a coward or is he courageous? Can one be both?

27. Do you think the samurai warriors would have been able to relate to Njal's and Bergthora's state of mind as honorable? Why or why not?

28. Discuss La Rochefoucault's saying that there is more of self-love than love in jealousy.

29. Who, in your opinion, is the morally worse person in *Fatal Attraction*: Alex, who is harassing Dan's family, or Dan, who was unfaithful to his wife?

30. Is there a difference between revenge and retribution? If no, explain why not. If yes, explain what the difference is.

31. Evaluate Ahab's obsession with Moby Dick. Is it reasonable to seek revenge on an animal? Why or why not?

32. Who claims that "Hell is other people"? Identify the author and discuss the claim.

33. On the basis of the story of "The Tail," do you think it is possible for children to feel existential anguish?

34. How might we say that Babette (*Babette's Feast*) maintains her authenticity and ego integrity through cooking a meal?

35. Evaluate Edward's healing process in *The Good Apprentice*. Has he achieved ego integrity? Why or why not?

CHAPTER 14
What Is a Person?

True/False Questions

1. Philosophy has now reached a clear and unambiguous definition of human nature. (F)
2. The inclusive method of defining human nature focuses on one aspect or definition only. (F)
3. All theories of human nature are descriptive. (F)
4. Nietzsche said that there are no facts, only theory. (T)
5. Any theory of human nature implies how we should treat those who qualify as humans, as well as how we should treat those who don't. (T)
6. A theory of human nature that holds humans to be weak and untrustworthy may develop into totalitarianism. (T)
7. A human being is always identified as a person. (F)
8. Kant claims that you qualify as a person if you are a rational being. (T)
9. Kant claims that any being capable of suffering qualifies for personhood. (F)
10. In the Christian tradition, animals should be treated with respect because they have souls, too. (F)
11. *Patria Potestas* is the right of the father to treat his family any way he pleases. (T)
12. A popular modern philosophical theory says that if you are capable of having *interests*, then you should have some *rights*. (T)
13. Capacity for speech is the only true evidence of suffering. (F)
14. Descartes believed that animals cannot feel pain because they are not self-aware. (T)
15. Peter Singer says we must assume that human and nonhuman nervous systems are fairly similar. (T)
16. Clever Hans was a philosophy student in Germany in the early twentieth century who impressed his professors by proving that animals cannot think. (F)
17. Kant's theory of personhood might include nonhuman beings who are rational. (T)
18. A slippery slope argument is an argument that undermines a position by trying to show that it leads to unacceptable consequences. (T)
19. Mary Midgley suggests that we evaluate the animal's capacity for suffering as well as its capacity for bonding. (T)
20. Animals are thought to have a higher capacity for suffering than humans because of their ability to anticipate future suffering. (F)

Multiple-Choice Questions

(Correct answers are marked with an asterisk.)

21. What is sometimes referred to as "the human reign of terror on earth"?
    a. the Nazi regime of World War II
    *b. humans' use of animals for human purposes
    c. the expansion of European Christian culture
    d. any government-sponsored terrorist group engaging in acts of terrorism

22. Who wrote, "In all our dealings with animals. whether direct or indirect, an ethic for the liberation of life requires that we render the animals what they are due, as creatures with an independent integrity and value."
    *a. Report issued by the World Council of Churches in 1988
    b. Jeremy Bentham
    c. Immanuel Kant
    d. Report issued by the Vatican in 1928

23. Who said, "The question is not Can they *reason*? Nor Can they *talk*? But Can they *suffer*?"
    *a. Jeremy Bentham
    b. Immanuel Kant
    c. Christopher Stone
    d. Mary Midgley

24. What does Christopher Stone suggest?
    a. that trees and other plants should have moral standing because they have rudimentary sensations of pleasure and pain
    *b. that trees and other environmental features should have moral standing because they are valuable in themselves
    c. that trees and other environmental features should have moral standing whenever they can be considered valuable to human beings
    d. that trees and other environmental features should not have any moral standing, since only humans can understand what morality is

25. There are three paths you can take in replying to a slippery slope argument. Which of the following is not one of the paths?
    a. You can abandon your original position, since its consequences seem unacceptable.
    *b. You can decide to ignore the argument on the basis of the moral character of your opponent.
    c. You can decide to dig in on the slippery slope and argue that there is a difference between your original position and the consequences of sliding down the slope.
    d. You can decide to take the consequences of your original position seriously.

26. Explain the difficulties of determining what a fact is.

27. What is the connection between ethics and a theory of human nature? Explain by using examples.

28. Who, according to Kant, qualifies as a "person" and who qualifies as a "thing"? Explain in detail, and evaluate.

29. What does Kant mean when he says we are not supposed to use other people merely as a means to an end? Explain by giving an example of using someone merely as a means to an end.

30. When an animal that has attacked a person is put to death, are we executing the animal? Explain.

31. Is it reasonable to seek revenge on an animal that has hurt you? Why or why not? Give an example of someone seeking revenge on a nonhuman animal.

32. Why is the concept of personhood important for the abortion debate? Can you think of arguments overriding the personhood question?

33. Discuss the case of Al the computer and Washoe the chimpanzee. Should the space station be closed? Why or why not?

See Chapter 20 for test questions relating to the narratives illustrating the question of personhood.

CHAPTER 15
Can We Decide Our Own Actions?

True/False Questions

1. Fatalism is not the same as determinism. (T)
2. Predestinarianism believes that, although all humans are tainted by the original sin, each individual can save himself or herself through good deeds. (F)
3. The theory of determinism is a normative theory of how humans ought to act with more determination and not be so indecisive. (F)
4. Modern science is primarily based on the principle of teleology. (F)
5. Behaviorism is a mentalistic theory according to Skinner. (F)
6. Skinner labels as "mentalism" any kind of theory assuming that human mind-activity exists separate from physical causes. (T)
7. The theory of determinism implies that there is causality in the physical world, but not necessarily in the mental world. (F)
8. It is a logical consequence of the theory of determinism that the strongest causal influence comes from the environment, not from heredity. (F)
9. In deterministic terminology, "environment" can also be called "nurture" and "heredity" can also be called "nature." (T)
10. In their effort to commit the perfect crime, Leopold and Loeb murdered a homeless man because they thought he wouldn't be missed. (F)
11. At the trial of Leopold and Loeb, the lawyer for the defense, Clarence Darrow, argued that existence precedes essence; in other words, we always have free will. (F)
12. Darrow's defense of Loeb was based on the idea that Loeb was not responsible for his acts because he was a victim of circumstances. (T)
13. Compatibilism believes that free will and determinism are compatible. (T)
14. According to Clarence Darrow, "Actions are commonly regarded as involuntary when they are performed (a) under compulsion and (b) as the result of ignorance." (F)
15. Soft determinism is the same as compatibilism. (T)
16. For Sartre, the human form of existence is comparable to that of a paper knife in the mind of God: For both, essence comes before existence. (F)
17. By saying that we are "responsible for all men," Sartre is saying that we are all socially responsible for the welfare of others and should be taxed accordingly. (F)
18. It is sometimes claimed that Darwin's concept of "survival of the fittest" is a tautology. (T)
19. Darwin believed that humanity was evolving toward a higher moral goal. (T)
20. Darwin believed that humanity was evolving toward an extreme form of selfish survival orientation. (F)

21. Ardrey's theory of human nature is an example of what is called sociobiology. (T)

22. Ardrey believes that humans have evolved successfully because we are aggressive and have a natural tendency to improve on our weapons. (T)

23. Ardrey's calling one of his chapters in *African Genesis* "Cain's Children" implies that Ardrey believes we are all physically descendants of Adam and Eve. (F)

24. The naturalistic fallacy: Jumping from a normative theory about what people ought to do to a descriptive theory about what people actually do. (F)

25. Richard Leakey is a strong supporter of Ardrey's viewpoint that humans are born aggressive. (F)

26. According to many modern scholars, the invention of the basket is a stronger cultural catalyst than the invention of the weapon. (T)

27. Richard Leakey's studies of several decades of chimpanzee life in the Gombe have yielded valuable information. (F)

Multiple-Choice Questions

(Correct answers are marked with an asterisk.)

28. Which phrase is applicable to determinism?
    a. 100 percent knowledge gives 100 percent accuracy in prediction and control.
    b. Everything is determined by one's heredity, or one's environment, or both.
    c. There is no free will.
    *d. All of the above

29. Who is primarily associated with the theory of behaviorism?
    a. Kant
    *b. Skinner
    c. Darwin
    d. Sartre

30. Who wrote, "Actions are commonly regarded as involuntary when they are performed (a) under compulsion and (b) as the result of ignorance"?
    a. Clarence Darrow
    b. Jean-Paul Sartre
    c. Robert Ardrey
    *d. Aristotle

31. What does Sartre mean by saying that "existence comes before essence"? Pick the most likely answer.
    *a. There is no human nature.
    b. Existence is essential to human nature.
    c. The only way you know you exist is to tell yourself that you are thinking.
    d. Trick question: Sartre says that "essence comes before existence."

32. What does Sartre imply when he says that "we are responsible for all men"?
    a. We are all socially responsible for the welfare of others and should be taxed accordingly.
    b. If you are a good Christian, you accept the idea that you are personally responsible for your neighbor.
    *c. When we make choices we automatically set ourselves up as role models for everyone else.
    d. Actually, women are responsible for all women, and men are responsible for all men.

33. Identify a straw man argument:
    a. an argument which claims that your opponent is a "straw man," someone who can't think rationally
    b. the same as the naturalistic fallacy
    *c. an argument that invents a viewpoint which is easy to knock down, and proceeds to argue against it
    d. the famous argument (quarrel) between the Scarecrow and the Wizard of Oz

34. What is the naturalistic fallacy?
    *a. jumping from a descriptive theory about what people do to a normative, theory about what they ought to do
    b. jumping from a normative theory about what people ought to do to a descriptive theory about what people actually do
    c. assuming that people are naturally good
    d. assuming that naturalists are more natural than other people

35. Who is the scholar who has studied the chimpanzees of Gombe for decades?
    a. Richard Leakey
    *b. Jane Goodall
    c. Robert Ardrey
    d. Konrad Lorenz

Essay Questions

36. Explain the significance of the story of Death meeting the servant at the marketplace.
37. Give an example of a teleological explanation.
38. Describe the theory of determinism in as much detail as you can, and give some examples of how determinism can be used to explain specific cases or situations.
39. Explain Sartre's example with the young man who has to decide whether to join the French resistance movement. What is Sartre trying to say?
40. Discuss Sartre's philosophy that there is no such thing as having to follow an order. Can you think of situations in which you would consider it necessary to follow an order you find morally objectionable?
41. Which, in your opinion, is the most important cultural invention, the weapon or the basket? Why?

See Chapter 20 for test questions relating to the narratives illustrating the questions of determinism, free will, and sociobiology.

CHAPTER 16
Different Gender, Different Nature, Different Ethic?

True/False Questions

1. There is a strong movement in the academic world to get rid of gender-neutral language in favor of gender-specific language. (F)
2. Research has shown that women's sphere of influence has been historically limited to the private sector because they are biologically incapable of contributing significantly to the public sector. (F)
3. Some philosophers believe that women's rational capabilities don't measure up to those of men. (T)
4. Aristotle believed that the female is like a deformed male. (T)
5. Plato believed that both men and women should be allowed to perform whatever function they are best at. (T)
6. Saint Augustine believed that since both men and women are created in the image of God, God must be part woman. (F)
7. Kant is one of the early champions of women's rights on the basis of his belief that men and women have the same intellectual capabilities. (F)
8. Rousseau insists that while boys should be raised with few restrictions, girls should be taught to please and help their future husbands. (T)
9. Nietzsche was a misogynist. (T)
10. A misogynist is a person who disapproves of interracial marriages. (F)
11. Wollstonecraft argues that if the only thing girls are taught is how to seduce a man in order to acquire a husband, then they are not well equipped for married life. (T)
12. Mary Wollstonecraft was an eighteenth-century spokesperson for women's rights. (T)
13. John Stuart Mill was a nineteenth-century spokesperson for women's rights. (T)
14. Mill wrote, "The modern individual family is founded on the open or concealed domestic slavery of the wife. . . . Within the family [the husband] is the bourgeois, and the wife represents the proletariat." (F)
15. Classical feminism was primarily concerned with the right for women to an equal share in the man's world. (T)
16. Classical feminism sees men and women as fundamentally different. (F)
17. One of the major events in the development of women's rights was World War I, when women had to take over men's work on the homefront. (T)
18. Simone de Beauvoir believes that if boys and girls are given a nonsexist education, they will become basically similar persons; gender differences are all a matter of environment. (T)
19. Monoandrogynism argues that homosexuality is preferable to heterosexuality. (F)

20. An ultra-radical version of androgynism suggests changing human biology to eliminate gender differences. (T)

21. Scholars have pointed out that research into human nature has until recently focused on the male as the normal human being. (T)

22. Gilligan suggests that male and female moral values are fundamentally similar. (F)

23. Deborah Tannen suggests that men and women may find it hard to communicate because they grow up having different speech patterns. (T)

Multiple-Choice Questions

(Correct answers are marked with an asterisk.)

24. Who wrote, "A woman who has her head full of Greek . . . or carries on fundamental controversies about mechanics . . . might as well have a beard"?
    *a. Immanuel Kant
    b. Jean-Jacques Rousseau
    c. Mary Wollstonecraft
    d. Friedrich Nietzsche

25. Who wrote, "Woman has much reason for shame; so much pedantry, superficiality, schoolmarmishness, petty presumption, petty licentiousness, and immodesty is concealed in woman—one needs only study her behavior with children!'"?
    a. Simone de Beauvoir
    b. Jean-Jacques Rousseau
    c. Mary Wollstonecraft
    *d. Friedrich Nietzsche

26. Who wrote, "Man shall be trained for war, and woman for the recreation of the warrior: all else is folly"?
    a. Immanuel Kant
    b. Jean-Jacques Rousseau
    c. Mary Wollstonecraft
    *d. Friedrich Nietzsche

27. Who wrote, "The faculties common to the sexes are not equally shared between them, but take them all in all, they are well balanced. The more womanly a woman is, the better. Whenever she exercises her own proper powers she gains by it; when she tries to usurp ours she becomes our inferior"?
    a. Immanuel Kant
    b. Mary Wollstonecraft
    *c. Jean-Jacques Rousseau
    d. Friedrich Nietzsche

28. Who wrote, "I wish to persuade women to endeavor to acquire strength, both of mind and body, and to convince them that the soft phrases, susceptibility of heart, delicacy of sentiment, and refinement of taste, are almost synonymous with epithets of weakness"?
    a. John Stuart Mill
    b. Simone de Beauvoir
    *c. Mary Wollstonecraft
    d. Carol Gilligan

29. What is Heinz's dilemma?
    *a. Heinz's wife is sick, and he has no money for medication. Should he steal the drugs she needs?
    b. Heinz's wife has had an affair with another man, and he has to decide whether to file for divorce.
    c. Heinz's wife has stolen drugs. Should he tell the police?
    d. Heinz is in love with another woman. Should he tell his wife?

30. How does Gilligan evaluate Amy's solution to Heinz's dilemma?
    a. Amy is confused and has not understood that saving a life is more important than keeping the law.
    b. Amy is confused and has not understood that keeping the law is more important than saving a life.
    *c. Boys tend to think in terms of justice, and girls in terms of caring, and Jake's and Amy's answers are both right, each in their own way.
    d. Amy has understood the situation perfectly, and Jake has misunderstood everything, because men always misunderstand everything.

Essay Questions

31. Give an example of a gender-specific expression, and substitute with a gender-neutral expression.
32. What does Beauvoir mean by saying that the only way for a woman to become authentic is to leave her role as "deviant"?
33. What is the difference between monoandrogyny and polyandrogyny?
34. In your view, are men and women fundamentally different or basically similar if given a nonsexist type of education? Your answer should include a brief description of Beauvoir's and Gilligan's theories.

See Chapter 20 for test questions relating to the narratives illustrating gender issues.

CHAPTER 17
Are We Good or Evil from the Beginning?

True/False Questions

1. The original sin is the first sin after one has entered puberty. (F)
2. Saint Augustine believed that humans have no free will. (F)
3. The Fall has become a metaphor for losing the innocence of childhood when one enters puberty. (T)
4. Many cultures blame woman for being the cause of the loss of an original human immortality. (T)
5. Elaine Pagels claims that the reason why so many cultures choose to see humans as guilty is that humans actually are guilty of losing access to Eden. (F)
6. Elaine Pagels sees the story of the Fall and Redemption as an example of anthropocentrism. (T)
7. The metaphysical theory of materialism states that material gain is the only true value in life; spiritual values should not be considered important. (F)
8. The metaphysical theory of dualism opens up for the possibility of the immortality of the soul. (T)
9. The term "the ghost in the machine" refers to someone having a mental problem. (F)
10. Thomas Hobbes was a materialist, a determinist, and a psychological egoist. (T)
11. Hobbes is the first thinker to express the theory that society is based on an agreement between self-interested people. (F)
12. Hobbes's social contract implies that the citizens must obey the sovereign under all circumstances. (F)
13. Hobbes's social contract theory can be seen as an argument in favor of monarchy. (T)
14. Rousseau believes that humans choose to agree on a social contract because life in the state of nature is, in his own words, "solitary, poor, nasty, brutish, and short." (F)
15. For Rousseau, everything natural is good in itself, and the more civilized people become the more corrupted they are. (T)
16. Rousseau believes that humans are naturally self-centered and that only proper education will create a compassionate person. (F)
17. Rousseau's theory makes possible the tradition of representational democracy. (F)
18. The "masters of suspicion" are Rousseau, Nietzsche, and Marx. (F)
19. Nietzsche disapproved of his sister Elisabeth's anti-Semitic views. (T)
20. For Nietzsche, slave-morality and herd-morality are the same. (T)

21. Nietzsche's transvaluation of values: Humanity has grown evil and sinful, and it is time for a return to family values. (F)

22. Nietzsche's concept of the Overman implies a future master race of genetically pure humans ruling the rest of humanity. (F)

Multiple-Choice Questions

(Correct answers are marked with an asterisk.)

23. Which phrase describes epiphenomenalism most accurately?
    a. Epiphenomenalism is a theory that reality consists of mental images only; the material world is an illusion.
    *b. Epiphenomenalism is a theory that mental images are a byproduct of brain activity.
    c. Epiphenomenalism is a theory that argues for the existence of extrasensory perception (ESP).
    d. Epiphenomenalism is a theory that God periodically intervenes and synchronizes the mental and the physical worlds.

24. What is the "ghost in the machine"?
    *a. a term for the mind-body problem
    b. the same as "bats in the belfrey"
    c. a term for Nietzsche's theory of the eternal return
    d. a term for the problem of controlling one's desires

25. What is the state of nature?
    a. Alaska
    *b. a presocial condition
    c. a prenatal condition
    d. New Mexico

26. In Hobbes's view there is physical equality in the state of nature. Why?
    a. because in nature humans are all physically fit
    *b. because the strong can kill the weak, but the weak can band together and kill the strong
    c. because the law of nature sees to it that nobody feels left out
    d. Trick question. Hobbes thinks that humans are physically unequal in the state of nature.

27. There are four levels to the view that whatever is natural is evil. Which of the following is not mentioned in the text?
    a. A practical level: Nature can be dangerous.
    b. A psychological level: If nature is evil, so are human passions and desires.
    *c. A philosophical level: It isn't natural to think rationally.
    d. A theological level: Humans must tame nature, because that is their God-given task.

28. There are four levels to the view that whatever is natural is good. Find the one that is not mentioned in the text.
   *a. A scientific level: Early science must be more correct than contemporary science.
   b. A historical level: Early human cultures are considered closer to nature and thus better than contemporary civilization.
   c. A psychological level: It is acceptable to feel and display emotions.
   d. An ethical level: Nature, and those close to nature such as children and animals, represent moral innocence.

29. The three so-called masters of suspicion are on this list. Pick the one who doesn't belong.
   a. Sigmund Freud
   b. Karl Marx
   *c. Jean-Jacques Rousseau
   d. Friedrich Nietzsche

30. Hegel believed that a slave may be a prisoner of the master, but the master is also a prisoner of the slave. Why?
   a. because the master must have a slave in order to feel superior
   b. because the master is in love with the slave
   *c. because the slave has some free time, but the master must constantly watch the slave
   d. because the slave may, on occasion, take the master prisoner in a slave revolt

31. What does Nietzsche mean by the "eternal return"?
   a. The soul will be reborn into another body, and the more ethical our lives are, the sooner we will escape the cycle of reincarnations.
   b. A criminal tends to return to the scene of the crime.
   *c. We have lived this life before and will experience it again and again, in exactly the same way.
   d. Unpleasant events and encounters keep repeating themselves, like "a bad penny returning."

Essay Questions

32. What does Elaine Pagels mean by saying that admitting guilt makes humans feel powerful?

33. Describe briefly the three major theories of metaphysics.

34. Compare Hobbes's and Rousseau's theories of the state of nature in terms of their similarities and differences.

35. Compare Hobbes's and Rousseau's theories of the social contract in terms of their similarities and differences.

36. Describe Rousseau's theory of humans in the state of nature, and compare it with modern attitudes toward nature.

37. Analyze Nietzsche's theory of master-morality and slave-morality. Which one might Nietzsche say that we have today, in the United States?

38. Describe Nietzsche's theory of the eternal return. If indeed he meant to make it a test for how much one loves life, could you pass the test? Explain why or why not.

See Chapter 20 for test questions relating to the narratives illustrating the subject of good and evil human nature.

CHAPTER 18
The Soul and the State

True/False Questions

1. Plato found inspiration for his theory that the only true reality is what does not change in the philosophy of Heraclitus. (F)

2. According to Socrates, people do things that are morally wrong out of ignorance. (T)

3. Plato claims that the soul has three parts: the Id, the Ego, and the Superego. (F)

4. Plato's charioteer tries to control two mules: one is lazy, and the other has a will of its own. (F)

5. Plato believes that society should consist of three levels: guardians, auxiliaries, and nobility. (F)

6. For Plato, any person aspiring to be a guardian has disqualified himself or herself by wanting the job. (T)

7. Aristotle was a proponent of slavery. (T)

8. For Aristotle there is no "state of nature" because the state is a natural phenomenon. (T)

9. The theory of natural law is a descriptive theory. (F)

10. There is an inherent contradiction in the fact that Marx was a materialist and that he criticized capitalistic profit-making. (F)

11. Marx is one of the three "masters of suspicion." (T)

12. A dialectic movement is a movement that develops through opposites. (T)

13. For Marx all cultural institutions are directly related to and determined by the underlying economic structure. (T)

14. The realization of labor is for Marx the moment where the worker realizes that he or she is being exploited. (F)

15. In Marxism, alienation happens when the worker loses touch with the product of his or her labor. (T)

16. For Marx, human nature is an unchangeable given: We are born selfish, and we will always be selfish. (F)

17. One objection to Marxism is that there is no incentive to work if everyone receives what he or she needs. (T)

18. The images and stories of dreams are what Freud calls "the manifest content." (T)

19. For Freud the latent dream-thoughts reveal that dreams are wish fulfillment. (T)

20. A mistake reveals itself to be a parapraxis when it reveals a hidden motivation. (T)

21. A parapraxis is a clinical term for a pathological fear of heights. (F)

22. The Oedipus complex is Freud's theory of a mother's unnatural attraction to her adolescent son. (F)

23. Freud believed that religion began with the young men ganging up and killing the Old Man of the tribe. (T)

Multiple-Choice Questions

(Correct answers are marked with an asterisk.)

24. Plato's political theory identifies three levels of society. Which one is not included?
    a. the working population
    b. the guardians
    c. the auxiliaries
    *d. the nobility

25. Who wrote, "Hence it is evident that the state is a creation of nature, and that man is by nature a political animal. And he who by nature and not by mere accident is without a state, is either a bad man or above humanity"?
    a. Karl Marx
    b. Jean-Jacques Rousseau
    *c. Aristotle
    d. Plato

26. Who wrote, "The soul rules the body with a despotic rule, whereas the intellect rules the appetites with a constitutional and royal rule. . . . Again, the male is by nature superior, and the female inferior, and the one rules, and the other is ruled"?
    *a. Aristotle
    b. Plato
    c. Sigmund Freud
    d. Friedrich Nietzsche

27. There are four key types of natural inclinations that are important to natural law theory. Which one doesn't belong?
    a. social existence
    b. procreation
    c. self-preservation
    *d. pleasure-seeking

28. According to Marx, each person in the communistic society is supposed to
    *a. work according to his or her ability and receive according to need.
    b. work according to a fair schedule and receive no less than minimum wages.
    c. work according to the dictates of the state and receive what the state deems reasonable.
    d. be self-employed: no more working for or with others, because it may develop into capitalism.

29. Which one of these is *not* one of the three blows to the human self-assurance?
    a. Darwin's theory of evolution
    *b. Marx's theory of surplus value
    c. Copernicus's theory of the heliocentric universe
    d. Freud's theory of the Unconscious

30. What is a parapraxis?
    a. a practicing Freudian psychoanalyst
    b. a paranormal experience in an everyday setting
    c. a clinical term for pathological fear of heights
    *d. a Freudian slip

31. For Freud, the ego has three masters. Which of the following is not one of them?
    a. the Id
    b. the Superego
    *c. the Self
    d. the external world

32. What is the "primal horde"?
    *a. Freud's theory of the beginning of religion: young men killing the old dominant male
    b. Marx's theory of the first stage in dialectical materialism.
    c. Aristotle's theory of the origin of slavery through taking prisoners of war
    d. Nietzsche's theory of the return of the master-morality with the Overman

Essay Questions

33. Explain Aristotle's theory of the four causes by using an example.

34. Explain Marx's concept of the realization of labor with an example.

35. Explain Marx's concept of self-activity with an example.

36. What is the Id? Explain and use an example to illustrate.

37. Compare Plato's theory of the soul with Freud's theory of the mind, and point out similarities and differences.

38. Identify the term *parapraxis* and give an example. Evaluate Freud's theory that there may be no mistakes, only parapraxes.

39. In your opinion, *can* we control our desires? Why or why not? *Should* they be controlled? Why or why not?

See Chapter 20 for test questions relating to the narratives illustrating the subjects of the soul and the state.

CHAPTER 19
The Storytelling Animal

True/False Questions

1. Alasdair MacIntyre claims that Western culture is morally depraved because it listens to the wrong types of stories. (F)

2. MacIntyre claims that we are part of a tradition and cannot divorce ourselves from our history. (T)

3. Narrative selfhood is not only a matter of personal identity, it is also correlative. (T)

4. To MacIntyre the narrative quest is a quest for virtue in a life. (T)

5. Aristotle was opposed to art, because it distracts the mind from its rational course. (F)

6. Paul Ricoeur is a nineteenth-century Belgian philosopher. (F)

7. Narrative time is the time period in which a historical or a contemporary novel is set. (F)

8. Hayden White explains that there is a fundamental difference between storytelling and history-writing. (F)

9. Perspectivism is the theory that what we call facts are really selections of data based on personal viewpoints. (T)

10. White claims that history-writing has not always been interested in finding out why something happened. (T)

11. For White, any narrative makes a moral statement. (T)

12. Martha Nussbaum agrees with most of the philosophical tradition when she says that emotions have no cognitive value. (F)

13. For Nussbaum we understand ourselves and our emotions best through narratives. (T)

14. For Nussbaum it is inevitable that since narratives reflect the values of society, narratives deprive people of their moral autonomy. (F)

15. When Saint Augustine was asked what time is, he answered, "When you ask me, I know—but when you don't ask me, I don't know." (F)

16. When our ego integrity is challenged, we can sometimes resolve it by reinterpreting the story of our life. (T)

17. Ursula LeGuin believes that telling stories is a form of life denial. (F)

(Correct answers are marked with an asterisk.)

18. Paul Ricoeur sees three levels to a story. Which of the following is not one of the levels?
    *a. The level of critical thinking: We distance ourselves from the make-believe of the story.
    b. The level of entertainment: We follow the story line chronologically.
    c. The simple plot structure: The story has to be credible.
    d. The level of understanding: Our memory repeats the order of events in reverse.

19. What is narrative time?
    a. the time it takes to tell a story
    b. the time period in which a historical or contemporary novel is set
    c. the age of oral storytelling before writing was invented
    *d. The reading experience of being immersed in the unfolding events of the book

20. Who says that novels "preserve mystery and indeterminacy"?
    a. Alasdair MacIntyre
    *b. Martha Nussbaum
    c. Paul Ricoeur
    d. Ursula LeGuin

21. There are several ways of dealing with challenges to one's ego integrity. Which of the following is not mentioned in the text?
    a. One might view the challenge as the hand of God, or of Fate.
    *b. One might choose to ignore the challenge and proceed as usual.
    c. One might view the challenge as being a consequence of something one has done, and feel guilty.
    d. One might choose to reinterpret one's life story.

Essay Questions

22. What is narrative time? Explain by using an example.
23. Nussbaum claims that philosophy has not wanted to deal with emotions because when humans are emotional, they are not self-sufficient. What does she mean by that?
24. Comment on Nussbaum's statement: "We have never lived enough. Our experience is, without fiction, too confined and too parochial. Literature extends it, making us reflect and feel about what might otherwise be too distant for feeling."
25. What does it mean that humans are temporal creatures, and why is this relevant for a narrative theory?
26. Comment on Joseph Campbell's remark that we wonder about the meaning of life only when we are having a bad time. Is he right? Why or why not?

27. Give an example of a rewriting of someone's life story following an identity crisis.

CHAPTER 20
Narratives of Human Nature

True/False Questions

1. In *Orphan of Creation*, the moral issue is whether Thursday is intelligent enough to be considered a person. (F)

2. The *Blade Runner* replicants are all unaware that they are artificial beings. (F)

3. In the end, Deckard (*Blade Runner*) is revealed to be another replicant. (F)

4. In "The Circular Ruins," a wizard creates another human being piece by piece in his dreams. (T)

5. In "The Circular Ruins," the wizard, in the end, turns out to be dreamed up by someone else. (T)

6. Pinocchio, the wooden puppet, has a problem: Because he is not human, he has no courage. (F)

7. Data's problem ("The Measure of a Man") is that he is not respected as an officer by his colleagues and friends. (F)

8. The underlying issue in "The Measure of a Man" is the ethics of considering some populations disposable. (T)

9. The story of the Ugly Duckling is an illustration of determinism: In the end it is the environment, not heredity, that counts. (F)

10. The story "The Flight of the Eagle" makes the same point as "The Ugly Duckling." (F)

11. "The Wild Child" is the story of a boy who grows up with no contact with humans, but who is strong enough to become king of the animals; in other words, it is the original Tarzan story. (F)

12. A very important question raised by the story of Victor (the Wild Child) in the eighteenth century was "Is some human knowledge innate, or is it all learned through experience"? (T)

13. The introduction to the film *2001, A Space Odyssey* can be seen as an illustration of Richard Leakey's theory that it was not the *weapon* but the *basket* that made humans intelligent, social creatures. (F)

14. In *2001, A Space Odyssey*, a black monolith is teaching a prehominid population to develop their intelligence by using weapons. (T)

15. In "The River of Separation," the conclusion is that men and women don't need each other. (F)

16. Alice Walker's story from *The Temple of My Familiar* is a pseudomyth about the early days when the First Men created both men and women. (F)

17. One of the key ideas in *Foucault's Pendulum* is that the meaning of life is the continuation of life. (T)

18. Thelma and Louise start their downhill slide toward a life of crime because of Thelma's overdrawn credit card. (F)

19. Stevenson's original story of Dr. Jekyll and Mr. Hyde tells of twin doctors, one good and one evil. Later versions made them into one and the same person. (F)

20. In "The Shadow," the scholar's shadow gains independent life and eventually causes the death of the scholar. (T)

21. In *Crime and Punishment*, Raskolnikov dreams of an incident when he was a boy: He watched a dog being beaten to death. (F)

22. In *Lord of the Flies,* Piggy is killed by Ralph because he tries to prevent Ralph from joining the gang. (F)

23. *Lord of the Flies* can be seen as an argument for Hobbes's theory of human nature. (T)

24. In *Dances with Wolves,* John Dunbar's task is to rescue captive white women from the Plains tribes. (F)

25. *Dances with Wolves* can be seen as an argument for Rousseau's theory of human nature. (T)

26. Camus uses the myth of Sisyphus as an illustration of the absurdity of life. (T)

27. Nietzsche tells a story of a young shepherd who bites off the head of a snake that has crawled into his mouth. (T)

28. In *Replay*, Jeff is experiencing a series of repetitions of his life and is bound to repeat every single action in his previous life. (F)

29. King Oedipus was attracted to the woman he believed was his mother, and this is why Freud uses the term *Oedipus complex.* (F)

30. In "Harrison Bergeron," anybody who is strong must wear a handicap bag, and anybody who is smart must wear a mental handicap radio. (T)

31. The story of *The Grapes of Wrath* follows the Mexican and Chicano migrant workers' struggle for political recognition in California. (F)

32. In *Atlas Shrugged,* the factory experiment showed that communism does not work because of human nature. (T)

Multiple-Choice Questions

(Correct answers are marked with an asterisk.)

33. What is the most important moral question asked in *Blade Runner?*
    *a. Is it right to create a race of artificial humans without giving them human rights?
    b. Is it right to hunt down people and kill them for money?
    c. Is it right for a detective to become personally engaged in his or her case?
    d. Is it right to create artificial animals without any concern for the environment?

34. Who wrote, "I saw that, of the two natures that contended in the field of my consciousness, even if I could rightly be said to be either, it was only because I was radically both . . . if each, I told myself, could be housed in separate identities, life would be relieved of all that was unbearable"?
    a. Umberto Eco
    b. Fyodor Dostoyevsky
    *c. Robert Louis Stevenson
    d. William Golding

35. In *Crime and Punishment,* what is the big question Raskolnikov asks himself?
    *a. Do extraordinary men have the right to go beyond the law?
    b. Why did the horse have to die?
    c. Is Kant right that the only answer to a moral dilemma is the categorical imperative?
    d. Is it morally acceptable to commit murder if the victim does not suffer?

36. Which theory can Golding's book *Lord of the Flies* be seen as an illustration of?
    *a. Hobbes's theory of human nature
    b. Rousseau's theory of human nature
    c. Plato's theory of human nature
    d. Saint Augustine's theory of human nature

37. Pick the author of this passage: "Courage, however, is the best slayer—courage which attacks: which slays even death itself, for it says, 'Was that life? Well then! Once more!'"
    a. Plato
    b. Elaine Pagels
    c. Albert Camus
    *d. Friedrich Nietzsche

Essay Questions

38. Since Thursday (*Orphan of Creation*) is granted personhood on the basis of her human genetic material, what would this solution entail for any nonhuman being petitioning for personhood? Evaluate.

39. Is Dr. Marchando (*Orphan of Creation*) acting in an ethically responsible manner by impregnating Thursday? Evaluate.

40. What statement does *Blade Runner* make about human nature and human rights?

41. What might be Borges's intention with the story of "The Circular Ruins"?

42. What is Data's problem in "The Measure of a Man"? How is it resolved?

43. Does Data have a soul, in your opinion? Do humans have souls? Why or why not? (Notice that there is no right or wrong answer here; the episode does not resolve the question.)

44. Could Data have duties as a Starfleet officer without having rights? Discuss.

45. What deterministic point does "The Ugly Duckling" story make? And what point is made by "Flight of the Eagle?" And why are both points considered examples of deterministic theories?

46. What does the story of the Wild Child suggest in terms of innate knowledge? Would you side with rationalism (define this) or empiricism (define this)?

47. Comment on the two Native American stories about the River of Separation: (1) Who is the likely storyteller, a man or a woman? (2) Is it a credible story? Why or why not? (3) What does each story reveal about the society, and are there differences between them?

48. What is the point of Alice Walker's pseudo-myth? Write a pseudo-myth in which men and women are created different, but equal.

49. What does it say about Stevenson's time period that Dr. Jekyll views his need for pleasure as evil?

50. There is a genre of stories in which an ordinary character has a *good and strong* alter ego. Give examples.

51. Compare "The Shadow" and the story of Dr. Jekyll and Mr. Hyde, and point out the similarities and differences.

52. If you knew that you would be experiencing your life over and over again (like Jeff in *Replay*), how would you feel about it? You may want to include Nietzsche in your discussion.

53. Did King Oedipus have an Oedipus complex? Explain by referring to Freud.

54. Discuss the story of "Harrison Bergeron," and compare it to the statement "All men are created equal."

55. Why might *The Grapes of Wrath* be interpreted as a socialistic story?

56. Evaluate the factory experiment in *Atlas Shrugged*. Is it a fair assessment of a communistic society? Why or why not?